Egyptology: The History and Legacy of the Modern St
By Charles River Editors

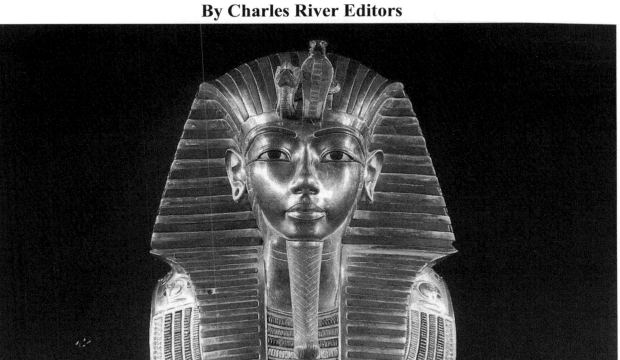

Carsten Frenzi's picture of King Tut's funerary mask

About Charles River Editors

Charles River Editors provides superior editing and original writing services across the digital publishing industry, with the expertise to create digital content for publishers across a vast range of subject matter. In addition to providing original digital content for third party publishers, we also republish civilization's greatest literary works, bringing them to new generations of readers via ebooks.

Sign up here to receive updates about free books as we publish them, and visit Our Kindle Author Page to browse today's free promotions and our most recently published Kindle titles.

Introduction
Egyptology

A picture of excavated ruins at Saqqara

"The genius of liberty, which made you, at her birth, the arbiter of Europe, wants to be genius of the seas and the furthest nations." – Napoleon's address to his soldiers before leaving for Egypt

Africa may have given rise to the first human beings, and Egypt probably gave rise to the first great civilizations, which continue to fascinate modern societies across the globe nearly 5,000 years later. From the Library and Lighthouse of Alexandria to the Great Pyramid at Giza, the Ancient Egyptians produced several wonders of the world, revolutionized architecture and construction, created some of the world's first systems of mathematics and medicine, and established language and art that spread across the known world. With world-famous leaders like King Tut and Cleopatra, it's no wonder that today's world has so many Egyptologists.

What makes the accomplishments of the Ancient Egyptians all the more remarkable is that Egypt was historically a place of great political turbulence. Its position made it both valuable and vulnerable to tribes across the Mediterranean and the Middle East, and Ancient Egypt had no shortage of its own internecine warfare. Its most famous conquerors would come from Europe, with Alexander the Great laying the groundwork for the Hellenic Ptolemy line and the Romans extinguishing that line after defeating Cleopatra and driving her to suicide.

Perhaps the most intriguing aspect of ancient Egyptian civilization was its inception from the ground up, as the ancient Egyptians had no prior civilization which they could use as a template. In fact, ancient Egypt itself became a template for the civilizations that followed. The Greeks and the Romans were so impressed with Egyptian culture that they often attributed many attributes of their own culture—usually erroneously—to the Egyptians. With that said, some minor elements of ancient Egyptian culture were, indeed, passed on to later civilizations. Egyptian statuary appears to have had an initial influence on the Greek version, and the ancient Egyptian language continued long after the pharaonic period in the form of the Coptic language.

Although the Egyptians may not have passed their civilization directly on to later peoples, the key elements that comprised Egyptian civilization, including their religion, early ideas of state, and art and architecture, can be seen in other pre-modern civilizations. Indeed, since Egyptian civilization represented some fundamental human concepts, a study of their culture can be useful when trying to understand many other pre-modern cultures.

Few of these things were on Napoleon Bonaparte's mind in 1798, when an initial review of France's naval forces led him to conclude his navy could not hope to outfight the power of the Royal Navy, which had been the dominant naval power for centuries. After months of planning, Napoleon crafted a scheme to attack and conquer Egypt, denying the British easy access to their colonies in India, with the ultimate goal of linking up with the Sultan Tipoo in India itself and defeating the British in the field there. Napoleon sailed with Admiral Brueys and 30,000 troops that June, heading for Egypt. Notionally part of the Ottoman Empire, Egypt was de facto a weak independent regime run by the breakaway Mamelukes. For France, it offered an overland route to India and a chance to beat Britain at her own game via economic strangulation.

Ironically, in their attempt to intercept Napoleon and the French fleet, Admiral Horatio Nelson and the British forces beat the French to Africa, failing to take into account their slower troop transports. While the British turned north, only two days later, on June 28, 1798, Napoleon's army disembarked at Alexandria. Back in Sicily, Nelson heard further reports about the French and again sailed south. This time, about 6 weeks after the French reached Egypt, Nelson's fleet destroyed the French Mediterranean fleet, leaving Napoleon stranded in Africa.

In addition to being unable to be reinforced or supplied by sea, his ambitions to establish a permanent presence in Egypt were further frustrated by a number of uprisings. Early in 1799, Napoleon advanced against France's erstwhile enemy, the Ottoman Empire, invading modern Syria (then the province of Damascus) and conquering the cities of Gaza, Jaffa, Arish and Haifa. However, with the plague running rampant through his army and his lines of supply from Egypt stretched dangerously thin, Napoleon was unable to destroy the fortified city of Acre and was forced to retreat. The retreat cost him almost all of his wounded as, harassed by enemy forces, he was forced to abandon most of his casualties to the Ottomans' mercy, or lack thereof. Most of the wounded were tortured and beheaded.

Upon returning to Cairo, Napoleon finally received dispatches from France which, with the Mediterranean rife with Royal Navy vessels, had been severely delayed. The dispatches told of renewed hostilities with Austria and her allies, and a series of defeats in Italy which had virtually annihilated all of Napoleon's previous hard-won gains in the Italian peninsula. Leaving his army under the command of his subordinate General Kleber, Napoleon took advantage of a lull in the

Royal Navy blockade and embarked upon one of his remaining ships. He set sail for France, where he would take absolute power within weeks of his return.

Napoleon harbored all kinds of delusions about his time in Egypt that were not based in reality, but he definitely left a lasting legacy in the region, one he would never live to see or appreciate. By shifting the theater of operations to Africa and the Middle East, Napoleon inadvertently ensured the Europeans would fight there in the future, and the French occupation impressed upon the locals the necessity of catching up to the modern world in terms of technology. Ancient tactics could not prevail against a modern army, no matter the numbers, but while that was a lesson Napoleon consistently taught his enemies in Egypt and the Levant to their detriment, the French also sped up the occupied populations' technological advances as well. Perhaps more importantly, the Egyptian Scientific Institute introduced numerous modern innovations, including the printing press, which in turn encouraged literacy. This brought about the emergence of nationalism and liberalism, leading eventually to the establishment of Egyptian independence and modernization under the rule of Muhammad Ali Pasha in the first half of the 19th century, and eventually the Nahda, or Arab Renaissance. In a sense, the French arrival in Egypt marked the beginning of the modern Middle East.

Though he couldn't have known it, the various scholars and scientists Napoleon brought to Egypt kicked off modern Egyptology, and a general fascination across the West. Until about 200 years ago the writing of the ancient Egyptians was an enigma to the world, but that changed when an ancient Egyptian monument known today as the Rosetta Stone was discovered (or rediscovered serendipitously) by French soldiers in Egypt in 1799. Now one of the most famous monuments in the world, the Rosetta Stone is a black granite stele that was inscribed with texts in Greek and two different scripts of the ancient Egyptian language: demotic and hieroglyphs. Stelae like the Rosetta Stone were monuments that ancient Egyptian kings inscribed texts on, usually to proclaim a battle victory or a legal decree. Since the kings who commissioned stelae to be built believed that the information they contained were important, they were usually large, as is the case with the Rosetta Stone. Although damaged over time, the Rosetta Stone still stands nearly four feet tall and over two feet wide, and it originally stood probably between five and six feet tall (Andrews 1982, 12). The discovery of the Rosetta Stone finally provided researchers with a way of reading the Egyptian language based on an understanding of the Greek translation.

As more individuals headed for Egypt and made more groundbreaking discoveries, the interest in Egypt heightened, as did knowledge about ancient history, despite the fact it happened so long ago and covered an immense span of time. Thanks to all these efforts, modern Egyptologists are able to learn an incredible amount about different periods through reading the surviving texts currently preserved in museums throughout the world and in the many temples and tombs in Egypt.

Egyptology: The History and Legacy of the Modern Study of Ancient Egypt chronicles how Egyptology as a discipline emerged in the 19th century, and its most important findings. Along with pictures depicting important people, places, and events, you will learn about Egyptology like never before.

Egyptology: The History and Legacy of the Modern Study of Ancient Egypt

A Different Kind of Objective

"Geography, topography, agriculture, hydrography, commerce and manufacture were necessary areas of inquiry for successful colonization. Specialists who could study the various ethnic populations of Egypt, and interpreters were crucial to the French conquest of Egypt. Scientists, artists, architects, and antiquaries were needed to study the natural history and cultural legacy of Egyptian civilization." – Melanie Byrd

Military historians tend to regard Napoleon Bonaparte's Egyptian Campaign as a monumental failure, and when evaluated through the objective prism of a purely military operation, it is hard to see it in any other way. The expedition set sail from the French port of Toulon in the spring of 1798, entering into a realm which the British Royal Navy, as the greatest naval power then in existence, wholly dominated. That the French fleet should have been destroyed at the Battle of the Nile in August of that year, just a month after landing, should have come as no surprise, leaving plenty of analysts to wonder how Napoleon hoped that he could escape such an eventuality.

When it did occur, and when the French expeditionary force, the Army of the Orient, found itself trapped in Egypt, there was little hope in the long term that anything could be salvaged. Again, it is difficult to imagine that Napoleon, in planning this escapade, did not predict or offer up a coherent plan to rescue the military situation once the naval disaster had taken place. Having been placed in this situation, blockaded in on all sides and entirely cut off from reinforcement or communication, the ultimate collapse of the adventure was inevitable.

Perhaps Napoleon believed that a French invasion of Egypt to oust the tyrannical Mamluk military leadership would be so welcomed by the oppressed Egyptian population that the invasion would assumed an unstoppable momentum. No doubt he hoped that French republican values, modified somewhat by himself, would proliferate upon their own merits, and create overnight a republic in Egypt that would owe its loyalties to France.

However, no such thing occurred. The despised Mamluk beys, Ibrahim and Murad, were granted a legitimacy they had not previously enjoyed, simply by standing in opposition to the French attempt to usurp power. The grassroots population of Egypt, with very few exceptions, wholly rejected the French presence in Egypt, while the Ottoman overlords, far from embracing the French as allies in some anti-British and anti-Russian confederation, formed a coalition with both for the express purpose of crushing the French.

After the Battle of the Nile, Napoleon, with his diminishing force, fought to pacify the Nile Delta, the most populous region of Egypt, while dispatching expeditions east and south to run the fugitive beys to ground. With maximum force, he suppressed a rebellion in Cairo, and then the French fought a desperate, but hapless campaign in Syria to try and preempt the inevitable destruction of his army. When all seemed hopeless, and when new challenges and ambitions beckoned him home, he simply abandoned the army, passing off authority to his second-in-command after he left.

However, far from returning to France in disgrace, he returned a hero, proclaiming a victory that seemed plausible, and which was hailed by the hero-hungry French population.

Disillusioned by ineffective and corrupt Directory rule, he maneuvered himself into power, and within a few years he had advanced to a position that allowed him to be crowned Emperor of France.

Napoleon

How was it that Napoleon was able to achieve this? Much of the answer, of course, lay in his astonishing ambition and his unassailable self-belief, but plenty of credit should go to his shameless manipulation of the facts and an astute use of propaganda. Throughout his Egyptian campaign, Napoleon made shrewd and careful use of art and science to enhance his own profile, and the profile of the expedition. Even if the military facts of the expedition make for miserable reading, its contribution to science, and to the expanding body of knowledge, is undeniable.

As Alexander the Great did before him, Napoleon included on his expedition to Egypt a separate corps of artists, engineers, intellectuals and academics, the savants who gave the enterprise its intellectual and scientific ballast. From this emerged not only an enormous weight of academic and technical material, but also numerous works of art commissioned by Napoleon himself to commemorate his adventure, and to portray it in the most favorable light. In the absence of real-time news reporting, these hagiographic representations of him, supported by an undeniably weighty deployment of intellectual forces, allowed Napoleon to return from Egypt portraying himself as a victor. This was a victory not on the battlefield, but in the field of enlightenment, in human endeavor, and in the acquisition knowledge, Napoleon could truly claim success, even if it was farther from his mind than military objectives.

Indeed, from this branch of the expedition, the Institut d'Egypte was born, and from it the genesis of Egyptology as a specific branch of science. This was a profound achievement, the ramifications of which are still being felt to this day. Whether by design or happenstance, Napoleon was certainly able to lay claim to this great triumph, and in the absence of much to show for his military outlay, he tended to promote this cultural imperialism, and all that it achieved, as a great leap forward for France.

Commission des Sciences et des Arts

"I am only at the beginning of the course I must run. Do you imagine that I triumph in Italy in order to aggrandize the pack of lawyers who form the Directory, …? What an idea! ... Let the Directory try to take the command from me, and they will see who is master. The nation must have a chief, and a chief rendered illustrious by glory." – Napoleon

What actually motivated Napoleon to undertake a parallel scientific mission is as elusive and enigmatic as the man himself. His apologists have asserted that when he was directed to undertake his invasion of Egypt, he saw it as an opportunity to make Egypt, an ancient land that had a profound influence on Western Civilization, a province of the greatest nation in Europe. More than that, they claim, Napoleon wanted to arrive in Egypt bearing the gift of modern science, the tool by which he would raise the modern Egyptians back up to the standard of their forebears. In the process, the French would map their borders, manage the Nile, raise their agricultural and industrial output, and reinvigorate their intellectual heritage.

Others who have been less charitable view it as a massive propaganda arm of the invasion, while still others consider it no more than a grandiose mimicking of Alexander the Great, who campaigned with a corps artists, engineers, writers and intellectuals. It was this, after all, that separated the likes of Alexander and Napoleon from the barbarian hordes, whose mindless destruction stamped their conquests with the irrationality of the philistine.

All of these were probably partly true, but it's only fair to point out Napoleon was acting under the impetus of his political masters, and while only a handful of bureaucrats were aware of what his mission comprised, those who did saw fit to recruit the necessary corps of experts to undertake the scientific work.

Napoleon was not personally remote from the interests and work of the experts either. It must be remembered that he trained as a military engineer, and that he excelled at mathematics. He was an avid reader of history, extremely well-informed, and although modestly educated, he was knowledgeable. In 1897, for example, he was elected to membership of the Institut de France, the most august association of learned men in republican France. He was, therefore, much more of a renaissance man than he was a pure military practitioner, and it would be wrong to assume that the composition of the Commission des Sciences et des Arts was of no interest to him.

Indeed, he was deeply interested, both for the sake of his own edification and for the gravity of his expedition.

Naturally, Napoleon had plenty of other things on his mind as the departure to Egypt loomed, so he delegated the practical work of setting up the Commission to three close colleagues: Gaspard Monge, a mathematician; Claude-Louis Berthollet, a chemist; and Joseph Fourier, a mathematician. The commission was formally established on March 16, 1798, more or less on the eve of the expedition's departure. Upon its inauguration, it consisted of 167 members, although 16 of these did not ultimately embark for Egypt. More than half were engineers and technicians, and in the end, the full list comprised 21 mathematicians, 3 astronomers, 17 civil engineers, 13 naturalists, mining engineers and geographers, 3 gunpowder engineers, 4 architects, 8 artists, 10 mechanical artists, 1 sculptor, 15 interpreters, 10 men of letters, and 22 printers in Latin, Greek and Arabic characters. Once it had been assembled, and once it met his approval, Napoleon organized the Commission along military lines, assigning each member a military rank, and an ancillary role associated with the practicalities of a military occupation. There were those, for example, who were responsible for supply, for commissariat, and for billeting and transport, among other duties.

Monge

Berthollet

Fourier

Although lengthy, the list of savants was dominated by just a handful of established and respected scientists, while the remainder tended to comprise young and eager graduates recruited from institutions like the École Polytechnique, the École des Ponts et Chaussées, and the École des Mines. In all probability, the sheer secrecy of the mission, whose objectives were kept from all but a handful of senior Directory members and military officers, discouraged more eminent names from volunteering. As the fleet assembled in Toulon, this minor army of book-carrying intellectuals began arriving at the port with absolutely no idea where they were going.

The fleet, comprising some 400 ships, set sail from Toulon on May 19, 1798, with the scientific corps distributed among the various troopships and transports. One can easily imagine that as the Frenchmen began to speculate on their destination, and as it became increasingly clear that that objective was Egypt, the scientists would have been far more excited than the soldiers.

The Formation of the Institut d'Egypte

"The whole truth never appeared in Bonaparte's dispatches, when it was in any way unfavorable to himself. He knew how to disguise, to alter, or to conceal it when necessary. He not infrequently altered the dispatches of others, when they ran counter to his views, or were calculated to diminish the good opinion he wished the world should entertain of him." – Louis

Antoine Fauvelet de Bourrienne

After barely avoiding the prowling British Royal Navy searching for them, the French fleet landed in Alexandria on July 1, 1798, but as the ships began to disembark and unload, the *Patriote*, a transport ship carrying a large part of the scientific equipment, ran aground and sank, casting an ominous pall over the scientific branch of the expedition before it had even started. All of the savants landed unscathed, and after lingering in Rosetta and Alexandria while Napoleon and his army marched on Cairo, they began to filter out to commence their work.

Once Napoleon had taken Cairo, and the preliminary institutions of military government had been established, an Institut d'Egypte was founded, along the same lines as the Institut de France. The objective of this association was to provide a center for the coordination of the scientific work to be undertaken in Egypt, and a club or forum for the commencement of what would, in practical terms, be the inauguration of the science of Egyptology.[1]

The decision to do this was taken by Napoleon himself in consultation with senior members of the Commission while still aboard *L'Orient*. Whether by coincidence or design, the establishment of a headquarters and the formal delegation of duties were done only after the disastrous Battle of the Nile, at which point Napoleon was facing military disaster. The order was given to the chemist Claude Louis Berthollet and mathematician Gaspard Monge to deal with the practicalities, which they did. On August 22, 1798, Napoleon signed the Institute into existence, and two days later, the first meeting was held in the in the harem room of the abandoned home of a prominent Mamluk bey. Monge was elected president and Napoleon vice-president.

Though he may have been vice-president, Napoleon effectively chaired the meeting and lay out an agenda of projects of a practical nature. These included the design of a better oven to bake bread for the army, how to brew beer without hops, and finding an effective way to filter and purify the water of the Nile. The members of the Institute soon met in closed session and devised a program of their own, and before long a plethora of studies were underway. In short order, the Institute boasted a library, a laboratory, botanical gardens, workshops and growing collections of antiquities, natural phenomena and specimens. Academic papers soon began to appear, and these were published in a variety of journals, most notably *La Décade Égyptienne*, and soon the *Mémoires sur l'Égypt* was established as the official forum for publishing Institute papers. Eventually, many of the articles and treatises would find their way into the epic, multi-volume *Description de l'Égypte*.

The Canal of the Pharaohs

Bearing in mind Napoleon's fundamental objective of obstructing British communication with India, and promoting Frances access to the Orient and the Indian Ocean, the concept of linking the Mediterranean with the Red Sea was central to his thinking. This, of course, was no new idea - for as long as trade across the Isthmus of Suez was conducted, Egyptian leaders dreamed of somehow linking the Red Sea with the Nile, and thence the Mediterranean. Work began on the

---

[1] The building that the Institute occupied was located in the vicinity of Tahrir Square, the focus of clashes during the 'Arab Spring' of 2011. The building was burned and severely damaged, with much of its archive destroyed.

construction of a canal to achieve this as early as the Nineteenth Dynasty (1292 BCE–1189 BCE). The project sought to join the two oceans through an artificial canal of modest length linking a navigable stretch of the Nile to the Bitter Lakes, and then to the Red Sea.

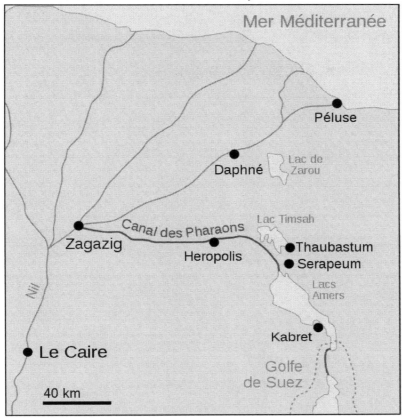

Annie Brocolie's map of the Canal of the Pharaohs

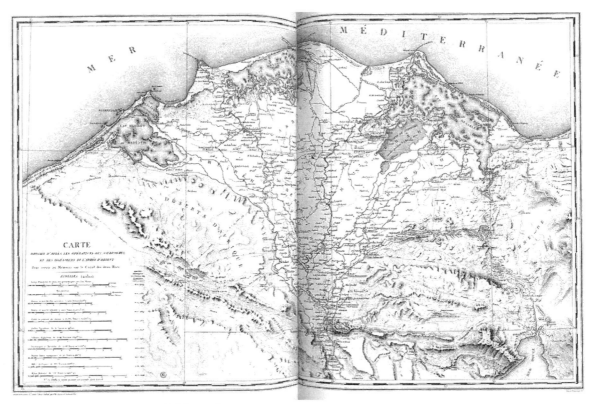

A French map produced for the project

There is no evidence that this canal, known as the Canal of the Pharaohs, ever came into use, or that ancient engineers managed to overcome the challenge of silting, but the project was a work in progress for several generations. It was abandoned eventually, but the idea was resumed under the rule of the Ptolemies, and ancient historians claimed the Greek pharaohs did succeed in uniting the two bodies of water. In the end, it proved impossible to effectively dredge the canal, and very quickly after it was flooded, it was chocked up by sand.

2,000 years later, however, Napoleon had at his disposal a corps of civil engineers surpassing any that the Egyptians had available, and principal among these was Jacques-Marie le Pére, the Commission director of "Ponts et Chaussées," or bridges and roads. Le Pére was ordered to undertake a topographical survey of the Isthmus of Suez, and determine by this the feasibility of a new canal, again linking the Mediterranean with the Red Sea via the Nile. After some investigation, Le Pére and his team of engineers were able to locate the route of the original Canal of the Pharaohs. It was found to commence at the Nile port of Zagazig, and then ran about 40 miles due east to the northern shore of the Great Bitter Lake. From there, an additional 10 miles or so of canal linked the southern shore of the lake with the Gulf of Suez.

On the surface, it appeared, from a simple visual survey, that along the route of the old Canal of the Pharaohs, the construction of a new canal would be quite possible. When a more detailed survey was undertaken, Le Pére came to the erroneous conclusion that a tidal discrepancy of some 30 feet existed between the Red Sea and the Mediterranean, which meant that if the isthmus was breached, Lower Egypt would be flooded. According to his report, without an extensive system of locks, the operation of any canal would be impossible.

History, of course, would prove him wrong, and in the end, ironically, a canal was opened in 1869 as a joint project between the French and British, the first such cooperative venture ever undertaken between the two previously bitter rivals.

Nonetheless, the question of a Suez Canal was interrupted by news of an Ottoman invasion building in the Levant. At that point, Napoleon was forced to abandon his sojourn in Suez and rejoin his army for a rapid march into Ottoman Syria, in an attempt to forestall a pending two-part invasion.

Maps, Mirages, and Mongoose

"From the heights of these pyramids, forty centuries look down on us." – Napoleon

While Le Pére was applying himself to the practicalities of a canal, the mathematician Gaspard Monge was applying himself to a phenomenon that caught his attention as Napoleon marched his troops across the desert from Alexandria to Cairo. In his efforts to keep the ultimate destination of the expedition secret, Napoleon had deliberately ordered that no water canteens be issued to the troops, lest it be surmised from that that the army would be heading somewhere where they would be needed. The result of this was a desperate march through lethal heat, during which the three divisions of his army suffered acutely from thirst. As they marched, men were tormented by visions of lakes spreading across the desert, only to disappear as they approached.

The word mirage is of French origin, and although numerous historical references to the phenomenon already existed, Monge was the first to attempt to come up with a scientific, optical explanation for it. His interpretation, after a great deal of observation and calculation, proved quite simple - a mirage, Monge explained, results from a superheated layer of air lying just above the sand, and this has the effect of bending light. The air density immediately above the surface of the desert is reduced by heat radiating up from the surface of the desert. The boundary between this heated layer, and a layer of cooler and denser air above, acts as a lens, refracting light from the sky back up to the cooler layer, and therefore into the eyes of the observer. The greater the temperature difference between these two layers, the more profound the effect of the mirage.

Monge spend almost two years studying this phenomenon before he reached this conclusion, and in 1800 he published his findings in the *Mémoires sur d'Egypte*. For decades afterwards, this thesis was cited as the original explanation of a phenomenon that continues to puzzle observers to this day.

While Monge was busy with that, 26 year old Étienne Geoffroy Saint-Hilaire, erstwhile chair of zoology at the Museum of Natural History in Paris, was charged with the responsibility of studying the fish and animals of Egypt. One animal that particularly captured his interest was the ichneumon, or Egyptian mongoose. His signature observation of the habits of this common creature of riverbanks was its tendency to eat crocodile eggs, and it was this that controlled the population of crocodiles. His sketches and observations were passed on to the artists department, where a small corps of illustrators set to work preparing the plates that would eventually feature in the massive publication *Description de l'Égypte*.

Saint-Hilaire

Anna Liflyand's picture of an Egyptian mongoose
One such artist was Henri-Joseph Redouté, the younger brother of the famous botanical

illustrator Pierre-Joseph Redouté. Henri-Joseph Redouté was in fact of Belgian origin, and he was just 32 years old when he commenced work on many of the finest illustrations featured in the *Description de l'Égypte*. He functioned primarily as a zoological artist, producing beautifully crafted illustrations that were later reproduced as engravings in the finished editions of the *Description de l'Égypte*. Occasionally, he was granted the opportunity to sketch antiquities, a job quite often designated to the various engineers, and several of his beautifully crafted monument studies also found their way into the *Description de l'Égypte*.[2] As was true for most of the savants, Redouté sat for a portrait sketch by another expedition artist, André Dutertre, and this portrait, along with all the others, was published in engraved form in writer and economist Marie Roch Reybaud's history of the Egyptian expedition.

Another prodigy whose career would be made by the Egyptian expedition was Marie Jules César Savigny, a 21 year old naturalist. Savigny interested himself mainly in the study of native birds, but like other members of the zoological staff, he found himself most interested in the ibis, which appeared to occupy a very significant place in Egyptian culture.[3] Not only did it appear in numerous bass reliefs and tomb paintings, but the mummified remains of ibis were unearthed by the hundreds.

J.M. Garg's picture of an ibis

The Greek historian Herodotus wrote that according to the resident Egyptians, the ibis controlled an annual invasion of flying snakes, and Savigny was intrigued to discover that most of the mummified ibis carried snakes in their stomach cavities. Having spent a long time studying the habits of the birds, Savigny realized that they subsisted mainly off shellfish and

---

[2] A great deal of the detail in the various depictions of antiques were contrived, and based on extrapolated detail, since most lay buried under centuries of sand, and yet others had been weathered or destroyed by the elements.

[3] In art, the Egyptian god Thoth was typically depicted with the head of an ibis. This was perhaps because the Egyptians saw the curve of the ibis' beak as a symbol of the crescent moon.

insects, and he concluded from this that the ancient Egyptians tampered with the facts to support their mythology.

In 1805, his opus, *Natural and Mythological History of the Ibis*, was published, appearing in print some time in advance of the main volumes of the *Description de l'Égypte*, which distinguished it as the first publication to appear based on work undertaken as part of the Commission des Sciences et des Arts. Trained as a botanist, not a zoologist, he stepped into the shoes of the far more eminent French zoologist Georges Cuvier, who declined to join the expedition.

Along with Geoffroy Saint-Hilaire, Savigny was responsible for most of the zoology sections of the *Description de l'Égypte*. The process of engraving the various plates took place between 1805 and 1814, and the final publication of the *Description de l'Égypte* would not be complete until 1822. The entire ornithology section of the *Description de l'Égypte* was contributed by Savigny, and he supplemented other sections on vertebrates. The invertebrates are represented on 105 plates with thousands of drawings, all of them from Savigny's research.

In all, some 2,000 artists and 400 engravers toiled to compile the illustrated plates that make up the final product, officially entitled *Description de l'Égypte, ou Recueil des observations et des recherches qui ont été faites en Égypte pendant l'expédition de l'armée française* (*Description of Egypt, or the collection of observations and researches which were made in Egypt during the expedition of the French Army*).

The book's frontpiece

The *Description de l'Égypte* would prove in the end to be the first and last great work that Savigny would undertake. As the bulk of the work was underway, he began to develop symptoms of a degenerative neurological disease. His speech and cognitive function was affected, and barely able to tolerate light, he wore a dark muslin veil to protect his eyes. His contributions to the final phases of production of the *Description de l'Égypte* were made through an intermediary, a young naturalist named Victor Audouin.

Audouin, of course, had never been part of the original scientific commission, and since he was unable to speak directly to Savigny, he was forced to identify and describe Savigny's illustrations based on secondary sources and the evidence of the drawings themselves. Savigny's own copy of the *Description de l'Égypte*, which has been preserved, is annotated with his many objections and corrections to Audouin's frequent mistakes.

In the meanwhile, to the northwest of Cairo, more or less midway between Cairo and

Alexandria is a rugged valley known as Wadi El Natrun, wherein lies a series of alkaline lakes. These lakes provided the ancient Egyptians with the sodium bicarbonate that was used in the process of mummification, and also for Egyptian faience. The lakes were later used by the Romans as a flux for glass making. Known as the Natron Lakes, they captured the interest of Claude-Louis Berthollet.

To the layman, Berthollet's study of the Natron Lakes might seem as dry as the region itself, and certainly his observations and conclusions competed unequally for public attention with the various treatises on antiquities. Nonetheless, he worked exhaustively on a detailed study of the Natron Lakes, and he eventually published his *Observations sur la natron* in the first volume of the *Mémoires sur d'Egypte*, adding in the next volume a more general treatment of the law of chemical affinities. His work was interrupted in August 1799 when he was summoned by Napoleon to accompany him on he secret return to France. Soon afterwards he was back in Egypt, which gave him the opportunity to complete his opus, *Essai de statique chimique*, published in Paris in 1803. This thesis is today acknowledged as the founding work in the systematic study of physical chemistry.

One of the most detailed productions of the Commission was a topographical map of Egypt, which comprised the final installment of the *Description de l'Égypte* published in 1828. It was originally intended that the map section of the *Description de l'Égypte* would precede every other section as a basis upon which to place and understand the incredible amounts of information, but in the end, the final product was so accurate and so detailed that the French military convinced Napoleon to not publish it and instead keep it sealed as a national secret. As a result, the map printed as the first plate preceding the antiquities volume was an outdated chart produced from historic sources by a French cartographer named Bourguignon d'Anville.

It was not until Napoleon's first exile to Elba, in 1814, that the engineers and cartographers responsible for the revised map were granted permission to publish it. 23 engravers were immediately set to work producing the sheets, beginning in the south of Egypt and progressing northwards towards the delta and the Mediterranean coast. Printed on the largest sheets of paper available, and challenging the printing technology of the period, it finally appeared as a supplement for the *Description de l'Égypte* in 1828. Locations and place names were listed both in French and Arabic, and the engraver responsible for producing the Arabic characters actually had a special course of training prior to putting pen to paper.

The final result, bearing in mind the extremely difficult circumstances under which the work was undertaken, was remarkable. A team of some 37 topographical and civil engineers worked under punishing time constraints, tormented by heat and sand, and often unescorted. This was the Corps of Topographical Engineers, led by 33 year old Colonel Pierre Jacotin, and it diligently compiled the necessary data. This even more impressive considering that most of the group's surveying equipment went down with the *Patriote* as the expedition landed.

Jacotin

The various teams measured off using chains and circle sightings made by the expedition astronomer, Nicolas-Auguste Nouet. Without access to accurate chronological readings to determine the longitude of Egyptian locations relative to the Paris Meridian, the coordinate grid used was based on a meridian passing through the tip of the Great Pyramid of Giza, and a latitude line at right angles to it.[4] It was found that everything could be plotted from these coordinates, which, in practical terms, confirms the precision of the original north-south alignment of the Great Pyramid. Its four sides are almost perfectly aligned with the four cardinal points of the compass.

The fieldwork was directed and coordinated by Colonel Jacotin, who then supervised the drawing of the maps and engraving of the plates for their eventual publication. The result was arguably the most precise and accurate map of any geographic location produced to date. It was (and remains) a masterpiece.

Baron Denon and the Antiquities of Egypt

"I felt that I was in the sanctuary of the arts and sciences…Never did the labour of man show me the human race in such a splendid point of view. In the ruins of Tentyra the Egyptians appeared to me giants." - Baron Denon

---

[4] The Paris Meridian is a meridian line that runs through the Paris Observatory now position, according to Greenwich Meridian at longitude 2°20′14.03″ east. Competition between France and Britain over the placement of the Prime Meridian was resolved only in October, 1884 at the International Meridian Conference held in Washington DC during which Greenwich was chosen as the international Prime Meridian.

Denon

Numerous studies were underway across the Nile Delta, covering almost every field of science, but the most rewarding and high-profile of these was the study of Egyptian antiquities, and that fell into the fortunate remit of Dominique Vivant, Baron Denon. Denon, a French artist, writer, diplomat and archaeologist, enjoyed the personal patronage of Napoleon, and throughout the expedition he was one of Napoleon's most trusted advisors. Indeed, it was at Napoleon's personal invitation that Denon joined the expedition.

Denon was a French nobleman and a personal friend of the French royals, and thus very fortunate to have survived the Revolution. Although his name was not officially included as part of the Commission des Sciences et des Arts, he nonetheless remained one of the most important members of the general scientific expedition.

Soon after establishing himself in Cairo, Napoleon sent the 30 year old General Louis Charles Antoine Desaix into Upper Egypt in pursuit of the fugitive Mamluk leader Murad Bey, and Denon was permitted to accompany the expedition as an artist and archaeologist.

Although it was a frustrating and inconclusive military undertaking, this expedition proved to be a seminal moment in modern archaeology. Denon's experience was recorded in his 1803 book *Travels in Upper and Lower Egypt: In Company with Several Divisions of the French Army, during the Campaigns of General Bonaparte in that Country* (*Voyage dans la Basse et la Haute Egypte*). This was arguably one of the most interesting and accessible publications to emerge from the entire expedition, and it comprises a breathless account of an academic and artist attempting to keep up with the furious pace of mobile military maneuvers.[5] Along the way,

Denon was the first European of the modern era to encounter, record, and draw the temples and ruins at Thebes, Esna, Edfu and Philae, prior to which the knowledge of Egyptian antiquities tended to be confined to the pyramids and associated monuments, and various other statues and stelae. When the expedition eventually reached Dendera (Dandarah), some 380 miles south of Cairo, Denon began to get a sense of the magnitude of what he was undertaking, and what visual treasures lay in store. He entered the gates of the city and was enthralled by the sight that greeted him. "I felt that I was in the sanctuary of the arts and sciences…Never did the labor of man show me the human race in such a splendid point of view. In the ruins of Tentyra the Egyptians appeared to me giants."

What Denon was referring to was the Greco-Roman temple complex known in ancient Egyptian as Lunet or Tantere. The rapid pace of military advances left him with almost no opportunity to sketch the ruins in detail, but he did discover a small, carved zodiac decorating the ceiling of a minor chapel on the roof of the complex, dedicated to the god Osiris. He would not have the opportunity to make a detailed copy of the object during that visit, but at a later point he returned, and he became the first to publish an engraving of the Zodiac of Dendera in his *Voyages*. The zodiac would be removed rather crudely in 1821 and transferred to Paris, where eventually it found its way to the Royal Library, and later to the Louvre.

Bernard Gagnon's picture of the temple complex at Dendera

Moving rapidly south, the expedition eventually reached Esna, and then Edfu, where Denon was again amazed to encounter the "sublime temple of Apollinopoli." The Temple of Edfu, dedicated to the god Horus, is one of the great temple monuments of Egypt, built during the Ptolemaic period sometime between 237 and 57 BCE. Denon would later describe the temple as

---

[5] Inevitable comparisons have been made between Denon's *Voyages* and the finished editions of *Description de d'Egypte*, and generally the former has been found wanting. Nonetheless, it offers a more easily digested version of the findings of the archeological work of the Commission.

the most beautiful in Egypt, and as he briefly toured the complex, he began to comprehend that, in architecture at least, the Egyptians appear to have anticipated the Greeks, and in his opinion, exceeded them. He made note of the unique column structures that appeared to borrow nothing, but utilized local themes of papyrus, lotus, palm, and reed for ornamentation. As best he could, he sketched what he found, but soon enough the army was on the move again.

The Temple of Denon

In early February 1799, at Syene (Aswan), General Desaix finally ordered a pause, and at last Denon was granted the leisure to tour, record, and sketch to his heart's content. He established a base on the nearby Elephantine, an island in the Nile lying just below the First Cataracts, from where he toured a treasure trove of monuments. A little further up the Nile, he discovered the island of Philae, which marked the ancient entry point into Egypt. "The next day was the finest to me of my whole travels. I possessed seven or eight monuments in the space of six hundred yards, and could examine them quite at my ease…I was alone in full leisure, and could make my drawings without interruption."

Among these, of course, was the famous Temple of Isis, but he seemed most captivated by the minor edifice of Trajan's Kiosk, a temple typically attributed to the Roman emperor Trajan but may actually date back to the reign of Augustus. Denon believed that if any Egyptian structure should be disassembled and returned to France as a sample of Egyptian architectural prowess, this ought to be it. He wrote, "It would give a palpable proof of the noble simplicity of Egyptian architecture, and would show, in a striking manner, that it is character, and not extent alone, which gives dignity to an edifice."

Olaf Tausch's picture of Trajan's Kiosk

By the end of February, Desaix abandoned his pursuit of Murad Bey, who seemed always to be just one step ahead. Thus, the column turned north and began to retrace its route back towards Lower Egypt. This offered Denon the opportunity to revisit and fill in the details of many sites and monuments that he had hurried through months earlier. He passed through Thebes three times, visiting again the temples of Luxor and Karnac, and in May he was at last able to revisit Dendera and sketch in detail the zodiac that he would make famous.

At about that time, Denon made contact with a second expedition dispatched up the Nile by Napoleon to conduct a hydrographic study of the Upper Nile. Under the direction of engineer Pierre-Simon Girard, this expedition, more formal in its arrangements, included a great many mixed Commission members. Upon examining Denon's illustrations, numerous engineers applied themselves to mapping the floor plans and elevations of various temples and monuments. This added a technical dimension to Denon's work that did not appear in his *Voyages*, but which did appear in the various volumes of the *Description de l'Égypte*.

Denon continued north with the army, briefly visiting the coast of the Red Sea before returning to Cairo in July of 1799. There he presented all of his observations, drawings, and sketches to the members of the Institut d'Egypte, and they too were enthralled, as was Napoleon. Two more expeditions to Upper Egypt were immediately authorized and dispatched for the single purpose of adding detail and substance to Denon's rather hasty records, and to determine by further search what else might lie waiting to be discovered.

These expeditions did not set off until August 1799, by which time Napoleon had left Egyptian shores, taking with him Monge, Berthollet and Denon. En route, Denon set about preparing his journal and his many drawings for publication. All appeared in folio edition in 1802, and for the first time, the French and European public became aware of the astonishing archaeological treasures of Luxor, Karnac, Philae, Edfu, and Dendera. The publication served to whet the French appetite for the full extent of the *Description de l'Égypte*.

The Zodiac of Dendera and the Rosetta Stone

"You tell me that I shall astonish the world if I make out the inscription. I think it on the contrary astonishing that it should not have been made out already, and that I should find the task so difficult as it appears to be." - Thomas Young

The zodiac

Upon the return to Lower Egypt of Desaix's column after its unsuccessful pursuit of Murad Bey, Denon was at last given the opportunity to study the large, circular planisphere, or Zodiac that he discovered on the ceiling of a stone chapel atop the Temple of Hathor. Although in almost complete darkness, he was able to complete a detailed sketch that later appeared his Voyage dans la Basse et la Haute Égypte, published in 1802. Soon afterwards the first members of the follow-up expedition arrived on the scene, and engineers Jean-Baptiste Prosper Jollois and Édouard de Villiers du Terrage, although working under similarly difficult conditions, produced a significantly more detailed rendering of the zodiac which would eventually appear in the fourth Antiquités volume of the *Description de l'Égypte*.

This version of the Zodiac generated a great deal of excitement when it was returned to Cairo. If accurate, it would reveal the position of the stars on the date that it was created, which would in turn offer an opportunity to more accurately date the construction of the temple, and since no one could yet read hieroglyphics, this presented a rare opportunity.

Thus, from the evidence presented by the two renderings of the zodiac, it was estimated that the date of its creation ranged from 12000 BCE, which was older than the world itself according to Biblical chronology, to a more modest 800 BCE. This, of course, was rather unsatisfactory, and some discord was generated among the savants arguing their various points.

In 1822, an antiquities thief by the name of Claude Lelorrain was commissioned by French antiquities dealer Sébastien Louis Saulnier to travel to Egypt in order to remove the zodiac and return it to France. This he achieved by a combination of saws, jacks and explosives, and in due course he arrived back in Paris with the somewhat damaged artifact. Saulnier then sold it to for the princely sum of 150,000 francs, and from the Royal Library it would eventually find its way to Louvre, where it remains on display today.

Its arrival in Paris created an even greater storm of controversy over the question of the actual date of its creation. Numerous theses and publications were offered up, with wildly varying speculations. Jean-Baptiste Joseph Fourier, for example, put the date at 2500 BCE, while Georges Cuvier placed the date at between 123 and 147 CE. It was Jean-François Champollion, an eminent scholar, philologist and orientalist, who accurately interpreted the hieroglyphic inscriptions around the zodiac and placed its creation around some time during the era of Ptolemaic Egypt, following the conquest of Alexander the Great. The zodiac is currently dated to the first century BCE, just before or during the reign of Cleopatra, the last of the Ptolemaic pharaohs.

However, by the far the most important discovery of the entire expedition was made by none of the savants, but by a military engineer attached to the army. Captain François-Xavier Bouchard was in charge of demolishing a section of the wall surrounding the city of Rosetta, or Rasheed in its original form. The French army, under the command of Colonel d'Hautpoul, was busy buttressing the defenses of the city, which lies on the westernmost branch of the Nile. It was the first substantive settlement after Alexandria taken by the French.

Built into a section of the wall was curious black stone of substantial size, inscribed with some written form of language, which Bouchard correctly assumed was of archaeological value. He reported the matter to General Jacques-François Menou, who in turn arranged for the transfer of the stone to the newly established Institut d'Egypte.

Picture of the Rosetta Stone taken by Hans Hillewaert

Now one of the most famous monuments in the world, the Rosetta Stone is a black granite stele that was inscribed with texts in Greek and two different scripts of the ancient Egyptian language: demotic and hieroglyphs. Stelae like the Rosetta Stone were monuments that ancient Egyptian kings inscribed texts on, usually to proclaim a battle victory or a legal decree. Since the kings who commissioned stelae to be built believed that the information they contained were important, they were usually large, as is the case with the Rosetta Stone. Although damaged over time, the Rosetta Stone still stands nearly four feet tall and over two feet wide, and it originally stood probably between five and six feet tall. The discovery of the Rosetta Stone finally provided researchers with a way of reading the Egyptian language based on an understanding of the Greek translation.

The texts on the Rosetta Stone were written during the reign of Ptolemy V in 196 BCE. Ptolemy V was descended from Ptolemy Lagos, who took control of Egypt after the death of his close friend, Alexander the Great, in 323 BCE (Lloyd 2000, 396). Like their pharaonic Egyptian predecessors, the Ptolemies ruled Egypt as a royal dynastic family, and as time went on they even assumed the traditional royal Egyptian titles of kingship. Although not one of the most important of the Ptolemaic rulers, Ptolemy V's reign was important for a couple of reasons. Most of his rule was marked by rebellion of the native Egyptians against their Greek overlords; no matter what the Ptolemies did to try to appear as Egyptians, they were still viewed as foreign by many who wanted to restore a native born ethnic Egyptian dynasty to power. A native Egyptian named Ankhwennefre led the rebellion against Ptolemy V, but it ultimately failed and was suppressed in 186 *BCE* (Chauveau 2000, 11). The Rosetta Stone, which conferred benefits to the native Egyptian priests, was commissioned 10 years later by the king in order to appease the important religious class (Lloyd 2000, 415). Other than suppressing that rebellion and commissioning the Rosetta Stone, Ptolemy V is perhaps best known for having Cleopatra I as his queen. Cleopatra I was the first of seven Ptolemaic women to have that name, and like her best known descendant, Cleopatra VII, she also briefly exercised sole rule over Egypt (Chauveau 2000, 4).

The historical importance of the Rosetta Stone as a primary source of events during a turbulent period in Egyptian history cannot be minimized, but its true importance was as a tool that scholars used to unlock the language of ancient Egypt. This was not lost on the Europeans at all, as the discovery and subsequent translation of the Rosetta Stone not only opened the door for the development of modern Egyptology but also proved to be an important chapter during the early 19th century. The possession of the Rosetta Stone and the race to be the first to translate it was such a matter of national pride that the monument became a pawn in the battle for prestige between Great Britain and France.

Under Article XVI of the Capitulation of Alexandria, the French were forced to surrender all ancient Egyptian antiquities, including the Rosetta Stone, to the British (Andrews 1982, 11-12). The British also had a number of scholars who realized the importance of the Rosetta Stone and sought to translate the enigmatic Egyptian inscriptions. Thus, the British government responded by moving the Stone to England, where it was officially donated to the British Museum by King George III in June 1802 (Parkinson 1999, 22). The Rosetta Stone still resides in the British Museum today, with the accession number EA 24.

While the British were in control of Egypt, they wasted little time collecting numerous Egyptian artifacts for their museums, and even after the British returned Egypt to Ottoman rule and the Napoleonic Wars were over, the French responded by sending several of their own officials into Egypt to collect antiquities. In particular, Henry Salt and Bernardino Drovetti, Consuls of Britain and France respectively, both deployed large teams of men to collect valuable Egyptian antiquities, which were then brought back to European museums in order to bring prestige to their nations. The priceless ancient Egyptian artifacts that were collected and housed in European museums became a sort of currency in the competition between the rivals, but the most important artifact – the Rosetta Stone – remained unreadable in the first couple of decades of the 19th century.

Knowledge of the Egyptian hieroglyphic script was vital in order to understand ancient Egyptian history, which was somewhat ironic because the ancient Egyptians were an extremely literate people. Compared to their contemporaries – the Hittites, the Babylonians, and the Assyrians for example – the Egyptians left behind a much larger and diverse corpus of written materials. Sacred texts inscribed in tombs, letters between private individuals, government census documents, and even erotic texts were some of the literary genres in which the ancient

Egyptians employed the hieroglyphic script. The Egyptians also wrote their texts on a variety of different media compared to their Near Eastern neighbors, including inscriptions on stone in tombs and temples, on papyrus for personal correspondence and documents, and on pottery shards known as *ostraka*. The ancient Egyptians' Near Eastern neighbors, who lived in places such as Mesopotamia, were usually stuck having to write their texts on mud-brick because stone was much rarer in their region and papyrus was nonexistent.

Some of the brightest minds of Great Britain and France gathered to attempt to decipher the Rosetta Stone, knowing that the person who successfully did so would not only bring great prestige to his country but would be immortalized like the long dead kings of ancient Egypt. The important difference between the Rosetta Stone and all other ancient Egyptian texts known to Europeans before its discovery was that it contained 54 lines of Greek text accompanying the damaged 14 lines of the Egyptian hieroglyphic script and 32 lines of the Egyptian demotic text (Quirke and Andrews 1988), while other known extant Egyptian texts only contained the hieroglyphic, demotic, or hieratic script. Since classical Greek was a well-known language in Europe in the early 19th century, if the Greek portion of the Rosetta Stone was translated correctly, and if it was essentially a copy of the Egyptian texts – which it proved to be – then the Egyptian hieroglyphic and demotic scripts could be deciphered by working "backwards."

Scholars quickly got to work and the first translation of the Greek text to English was done by Briton Reverend Stephen Weston in London in 1802 (Andrews 1982, 13). But even once that was done, the enigmatic Egyptian scripts remained to be deciphered. The first major studies of the Egyptian demotic script were done by Frenchman A.I. Silvestre de Sacy and Swede J.D. Åkerblad, who were able to identify the demotic version of some of the Greek proper names and place names in 1802 (Andrews 1982, 13).

Although these were great leaps forward in the understanding of the ancient Egyptian language, it would take several more years and the hard work of two men to finally decipher the hieroglyphic script. Despite the best efforts of other scholars, the eventual decipherment of the Rosetta Stone would be based on the efforts of men from the two opposing imperial powers of the time: Englishman Thomas Young and Frenchman Jean-François Champollion. Although the men worked separately, and in some ways against each other, each contributed invaluable insight into not only the decipherment of the Rosetta Stone but also the modern comprehension of the ancient Egyptian language. The two men never knew each other personally, perhaps owing at least partially to their nations' rivalries at the time, but they were familiar with one another's work.

Thomas Young

Jean-François Champollion

In less than 10 years, Champollion was able to determine values for most of the hundreds of hieroglyphic signs known at the time, both phonetic and idiomatic, and he was able to compile the first Egyptian hieroglyphic grammar book and dictionary (Griffith 1951, 41). Champollion's hard work had paid off; he had finally solved the riddle of the Rosetta Stone.

What Champollion did was truly amazing considering that even today it is often a standard requirement for graduate students of ancient Egyptian history to study the language for at least three years, and even then most experts will say that is only an introduction. Advanced scholars of ancient Egyptian language require a whole lifetime to master the language. Perhaps that is what makes Champollion's decipherment of the Rosetta Stone truly remarkable. He was a pioneer who traversed unknown territory, making his discovery without any precedents to work from.

After Champollion deciphered the Rosetta Stone and the entire Egyptian written language, he traveled throughout Europe to promote his findings. He also traveled extensively throughout Egypt, where sources indicate that he felt particularly at home. The warm arid climate of Egypt acted as a soothing elixir on his body, as Champollion suffered from a chronic cough, headaches, and shortness of breath for much of his life (Myerson 2005, 174). The scholar may have suffered from asthma, tuberculosis, or another ailment that is easily treatable today, but in the early 19th century it would have been a seriously debilitating and often deadly malady. He also appears to have felt a spiritual connection with the Nile Valley that eluded him in Europe.

Many other Egyptologists who came after Champollion would also feel the same connection with Egypt, but unlike many of his successors, Champollion would only spend a short time there. Champollion returned to France, where some of his influential friends in the government helped elect him to the Académie des Inscriptions in 1830, and one year later he became the first chair of Egyptology at the Collège de France (Griffith 1951, 44). These would become important positions historically, as they marked the first time that the study of Egyptology was officially sanctioned by a government. Champollion also became a sort of celebrity after his return to France; the pope and King Louis XVIII, who replaced Napoleon, met with Champollion and bestowed honors upon him. (Meyerson 2005, 266). Unfortunately for Champollion, he was unable to enjoy his professional success for long, because he died a few months later of apoplexy on March 3, 1832 (Griffith 1951, 44). Ironically, Champollion died at the same age, 41, that Thomas Young was when the Englishman had first begun his work on the Rosetta Stone.

Perhaps the biggest difference between the professional lives of Young and Champollion – and the primary reason why Champollion is known more today – is the level of publications produced by the two. Young published very little of his discoveries, most of which was published posthumously by others, while Champollion published and presented his findings whenever he could. However, Champollion never lived to see the publication of his Egyptian grammar book. In 1833, the French government purchased Champollion's unpublished writings from his widow and deposited them in the Bibliothèque Nationale (National Library) (Griffith 1951, 44). The only complete manuscript in the collection was his *Grammaire Égyptienne* ("Egyptian Grammar"), which was published posthumously in 1838 (Griffith 1951, 46). Jean's brother Jacques spent the next three decades editing and publishing numerous of his other works.

Tableau des Signes Phonétiques
des écritures hiéroglyphique et Démotique des anciens Égyptiens

Lettres Grecques	Signes Démotiques	Signes Hiéroglyphiques
A		
B		
Γ		
Δ		
E		
Z		
H		
Θ		
I		
K		
Λ		
M		
N		
Ξ		
O		
Π		
P		
Σ		
T		
Υ		
Φ		
Ψ		
X		
Ω		
ΤΟ.		

Champollion's side by side comparison of the corresponding Greek, demotic and hieroglyphic characters

Although *Grammaire Égyptienne* would prove to be the basis for all other studies of the ancient Egyptian language (and by extension Egyptology itself), Champollion's caustic and polarizing personality left many other scholars doubting, at least publicly, the credibility of his work for decades after his death. Because of his upbringing during the Enlightenment and the political turmoil of late 18th century France, Champollion was an extremely opinionated man who often ran afoul of important people and fellow scholars alike. For example, in 1816, the young Champollion was banished from Grenoble and his position at the university due to his unwavering anti-clerical and pro-democratic positions (Griffith 1951, 39). The French monarchy had been restored, and many of the political ideals of the Enlightenment, which Champollion championed, fell out of favor with the government. A large portion of Champollion's adult life was absorbed with political polemics, which naturally earned him many enemies.

Even when he abandoned politics in favor of full-time Egyptology and research, his career was still shadowed by the political enemies he made (Griffith 1951, 40). Although academic research is supposed to be pure and free from politics, Champollion's political opinions, religious prejudices, and national rivalries all contributed to opposition of his theories in the early stages of Egyptology (Griffith 1951, 45). And beyond his political opinions, Champollion brought at least some of the professional wrath on himself when he refused to acknowledge any debt to Thomas Young in the decipherment of the Rosetta Stone, which is documented today on the stone's label at the British Museum (Reid 2004, 41).

Widespread disagreement over Champollion's grammar theories concerning the ancient Egyptian language and his decipherment of the Rosetta Stone continued until another bilingual monumental inscription, the Decree of Canopus, was discovered in 1866 and confirmed his ideas (Quirke and Andrews 1988, 3). The Decree of Canopus also convinced scholars that the Rosetta Stone had not survived fully intact. E.A. Wallis Budge explained, "Now the Rosetta Stone is inscribed with 32 lines of demotic, and the Stele of Canopus with 73; but as the lines on the Rosetta Stone are rather more than double the length of those on the Stele of Canopus, it is pretty certain that each document is of about the same length. The Stele of Canopus has 74 lines of Greek to 54 on the Rosetta Stone, but as the letters are longer and wider, it is clear from this also that the Greek versions occupied about the same space. Allowing then for the difference in the size of the hieroglyphic characters, we should expect the hieroglyphic inscription on the Rosetta Stone to occupy 14 or 15 lines. When complete the stele must have been about twelve inches longer than it is now, and the top was probably rounded and inscribed, like that of the Stele of Canopus, with a winged disk…"

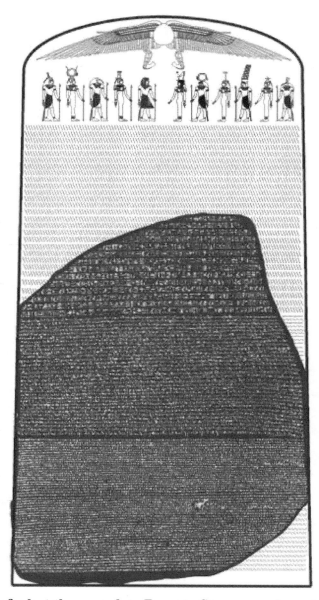

A reproduced image of what the complete Rosetta Stone may have looked like

The text itself ended up being a priestly decree, only a fragment of which has survived, since the original stelae would no doubt have been more than twice as large. The decree was issued at Memphis, then the most important Egyptian city, and it concerned the young king Ptolemy V Epiphanes of Egypt (205-180 BCE). It was the concluding sentence of the Greek inscription that, when translated, brought it home to the savants that the same text in three different languages had been preserved. That sentence read, "This decree shall be inscribed on a stele of hard stone in sacred and native and Greek characters and set up in each of the first, second and third temples beside the image of the ever-living king."

It would be impossible to overstate the importance that the discovery and decipherment of the Rosetta Stone has had. If the Rosetta Stone had not been discovered in a wall in 1799, Thomas Young and Jean-François Champollion may have never worked to unlock the enigmatic hieroglyphic script, and the history of ancient Egypt would have remained an enigma, possibly forever shrouded in mysterious tales of wonder. Since the ancient Egyptians left behind so many different types of written texts, understanding their language was integral to understanding their history. Although Champollion's *Grammaire Égyptienne* has been proven to be incorrect in many places, it provided the basis for all other subsequent grammar studies of ancient Egyptian language, and with it the establishment of the modern discipline of Egyptology. As grammatical knowledge of the language progressed, it was revealed that there were also different phases or dialects of the language. The different dialects of ancient Egyptian were Old, Middle, and Late Egyptian, along with Coptic, and subsequent Egyptologists were also able to discover that demotic was a spoken dialect as well as a form of writing (Allen 2006, 404). The knowledge of these different dialects of the ancient Egyptian language allowed scholars to move forward with even new discoveries.

In the 20th century, Egyptologists developed different, nuanced views of how the ancient Egyptian language's verbal system worked. British Egyptologist Alan Gardiner developed new theories about the ancient Egyptian grammatical system and eventually published them in the first modern Egyptian grammar textbook, *Egyptian Grammar, being an Introduction the Study of Hieroglyphs*, in 1927 (Allen 2006, 404). Despite its age, Gardiner's *Egyptian Grammar* continues to be used by grammarians and students of the ancient Egyptian language throughout the world, even as it has since been challenged by other theories of Egyptian grammar. Some linguistics, such as Jakob Polotsky, saw Gardiner's treatment of the Egyptian verbal system as too simple and thus began to develop more complex theories. By the 1970s, Polotsky's grammatical theories had attained widespread acceptance among Egyptologists, and they became known as "standard theory" (Allen 2006, 406). The "standard theory" of Egyptian grammar was then challenged during the 1980s, which led to the formation of yet another grammatical philosophy best exemplified in James Allen's grammar textbook *Middle Egyptian: An Introduction to the Language and Culture of Hieroglyphs*. Given that the study of languages is an art and not a science, a combination of the three grammatical theories can be, and sometimes are, utilized simultaneously. In the future, new theories of ancient Egyptian grammar will probably be developed and published as textbooks, but none of this would have been possible without the work of Young and Champollion on the Rosetta Stone.

Description de l'Égypte

The first official publications of the *Description de l'Égypte* began to appear in 1809, and releases continued for 20 years, when the final volume was published in 1829. The final product took 20 years of labor, which continued until long after Napoleon had departed French shores for his second exile in Saint Helena. Its objective was to catalogue and chronicle every aspect of ancient and modern Egypt, as well as its entire natural history. It was a monumental task that required the labor of at least 160 civilian scholars and scientists, as well as some 2,000 artists and technicians, among whom were 400 engravers.

The notion of creating a single, comprehensive compendium of the entire work of the Commission des Sciences et Arts d'Egypte did not accompany Napoleon to Egypt. In actuality, it was conceived as the weight of research began to build, and as plans were made to publish and disseminate it. The original concept was put forward by Jean-Baptiste Joseph Fourier, whose task it was to unite the papers and reports of the various disciplines, precisely for the purpose of later publication. By the time the French began to evacuate towards the end of 1801, a massive amount of written and illustrative material had been accumulated, along with a great weight of artefacts and specimens, most of which the British confiscated, but many of which were smuggled out.

It was Napoleon, already back in Europe in February 1802, who issued the decree that would see a commission established for the sole purpose of managing and organizing this extraordinary scholarly achievement and arranging it into a series of associated publications. Jean Antoine Chaptal, French minister of the interior, was perhaps the main instigator, but Napoleon had an obvious interest in seeing his Egyptian adventure immortalized in something as profound as the *Description de l'Égypte*.

Chaptal

Most of the material that eventually appeared in the *Description de l'Égypte* had already circulated in the journal *La Decade*, the newspaper *Courier de L'Égypte*, and the four-volume *Mémoires sur l'Égypte*, which was a development of *La Decade* published by the French government during and after the Egyptian campaign. In addition, a mass of notes and illustrations accumulated by the various savants required editing and engraving in preparation for publication, and in the end, at any point when a sufficient amount of material was finished and available, a volume was produced.

The initial 10 volumes of engravings were presented for the approval of the French emperor in

January 1808. The emperor, of course, was Napoleon, who in 1804 crowned himself such. After Napoleon's exile, subsequent volumes were published by order of the French king, and later simply by the government. The first edition, known as the Imperial Edition, comprised 23 volumes, and the second, known as the Panckoucke Edition, was extended to 37 volumes. It is not known how many of these were ultimately produced, or how many remain in existence.

On December 17, 2011, during clashes between protesters and the Egyptian army, the Institut d'Egypte was severely damaged in a fire, and it was reported that the original manuscript of the *Description de l'Égypte* was destroyed. In fact, the building was home only to a 23 volume set of the first edition, which was saved with only minor damage. It's believed that two more complete sets exist in private hands in Egypt, while the bulk of the original material that comprised the description is housed in the French National Archives in Paris and the national library.

Napoleon's Egyptian Campaign failed in all of its objectives other than in the acquisition of knowledge. Far from frustrating British ambitions in the Orient, the British triumphed in the minor war that Napoleon triggered, and it was the British who would dominate Egypt for the next 150 years.

Napoleon may have failed to take the Levant and failed to establish a French colony, but he certainly contributed enormously to the body of knowledge. The founding of the Institut d'Egypte began the science of Egyptology, and the *Description de l'Égypte* remains one of the great scholarly works of the age. The Empire style was founded, Orientalism became vogue, and ancient Egypt, one of the greatest of all civilizations, found focus once again in the Western consciousness, much the way the ancient Greeks and Romans inspired the Renaissance.

As for Napoleon himself, his ambitions would eventually lead him to Waterloo and bring him to the remote island of Saint Helena in the south Atlantic, one of the most remote corners on the planet. There, he would dictate his memoirs to his assistant, Louis Antoine Fauvelet de Bourrienne, who remained with him. In a state of disillusionment, he died on May 5, 1821, at the age of 52. Most of what he achieved in the short span of his life would be discredited by his enemies, but the era would carry his name, and *Description de l'Égypte* will always remain one of the purest and greatest achievements of his life.

A. Vol. V.   PYRAMIDES DE MEMPHIS.   Pl. ti.

VUE DU SPHINX ET DE LA GRANDE PYRAMIDE, PRISE DU SUD-EST.

Drawings of the Sphinx from Description de l'Egypte
Centuries after the fall of the Egyptian pharaohs, the knowledge of the chronology, religion, and overall history of ancient Egypt was entirely forgotten during the Middle Ages, with the exception of references in the Bible and those made by classical historians and geographers such as Herodotus, Diodorus, and Strabo. Medieval interest in ancient Egypt focused on the arcane

and esoteric, usually involving "magic," and had little to do with scientific knowledge (Burnett 2003, 89-96). To the people of the Middle Ages, ancient Egypt had little to offer beyond some possible mystical knowledge, and since modern archaeology would not become a field for several centuries, obscure references by classical writers to Heracleion and Thonis were ignored.

However, as archaeology and Egyptology would gradually become legitimate fields of academic study in the 19th century, there was renewed interest in Biblical verses and classical passages pertaining to ancient Egypt. 19th century scholars sought to use their new knowledge and methodologies to prove the historicity of such things as Exodus and Greek claims of Egyptian origins for many of their myths. Inevitably, as they carefully studied these passages, there was a renewed interest in unknown and presumably lost cities such as Heracleion/Thonis. Scholars endeavored to find these cities based on the few references available, but even the classical references that mentioned Heracleion/Thonis did little to help them find the city. It would not be until recently that knowledge of geology, weather patterns, and underwater archeology allowed for the discovery and study of the once lost city.

Archaeology, to take the term on its most commonly accepted level, is a discipline concerned with the past that achieves its outcomes through examination of artifacts associated with human manufacture or which carry evidence of human contact and interaction. While it is true that most archaeologists agree on these basic premises, the gradations of difference surrounding the key concepts are paramount. Archaeology is many things to many people and has a plethora of specialized subsets within it. Some examples include: Rescue Archaeology, Experimental Archaeology, Historical Archaeology, Industrial Archaeology, Prehistoric Archaeology, Processual Archaeology, Post-processual Archaeology, Theoretical Archaeology, Landscape Archaeology, Feminist Archaeology, Fringe Archaeology, Popular Archaeology, Consultant Archaeology and Biblical Archaeology, to name but a few key examples from a much longer list. Agendas, theories, methods and motivations will differ between the many archaeologists that take part in works crossing into these subset areas. An Industrial archaeologist looks at different time periods than a Prehistoric archaeologist, and a Post-Processual archaeologist has a different set of values, ideals and intentions than a Processual archaeologist. Even within these so-called groups individuals will disagree with each other regarding the nature, intention, best working method and theoretical approach to be taken as an archaeologist. One archaeological theorist named Johnson stated that these groups are "actually a very diverse set of concerns and ideas that coalesced around certain slogans" and the blanket overarching term is not a referent for uniformity, but rather "conceals a great diversity of viewpoints and traditions".[6]

Further differences can be noted with different cultural backgrounds, as with French, German and Dutch teams, for example, each having their own cultural approaches towards excavation techniques and documentation, being the result of training undertaken from a particular cultural background. It is often the case in sciences that key concepts are agreed upon but most everything else is fair game for debate and discussion. For some, archaeology is a kind of storytelling,[7] for others it is detective work,[8] to some an art,[9] to some a science[10] and to some

---

[6] Johnson, Matthew. 1999. *Archaeological Theory – An Introduction*. Blackwell Publishers, UK. pp 101.

merely a science of rubbish.[11] While there are those who have claimed in the past that archaeology is a subset of other disciplines, such as history[12] or anthropology,[13] such claims carry little weight in contemporary times and owe more to the origins of the discipline than to what it has since become. Archaeology is no more a handmaiden to history[14] than it is a treasure hunting adventure,[15] although the echoes of these early avenues and instances still color the discipline as it continues to develop. Archaeologist Chang stated that "as a tool archaeology serves many masters"[16] and it is important to remember that while one archaeologist may focus on reconstructing human actions of the past,[17] another may be more interested in large scale, long term material change traced through monuments, structures and settlement patterns.[18] Archaeology allows for multiple approaches, and considering the differing finds, conditions, challenges and contexts encountered on archaeology sites around the world different approaches, theories and intentions are very appropriate.

As the archaeologist Knudson stated, "archaeology is a complex, scientific discipline which encompasses many levels of inquiry and many varied goals".[19] As to the more philosophical questions of what archaeology is and does, each archaeologist will have their own point of view. Joukowsky is more personal when discussing the need for archaeology, stating: "the essence of archaeology is that it makes our world much more meaningful… Archaeology deepens our understanding of humanity and society… it uplifts us by satisfying our basic desire and need to know who we are".[20] This deals with the philosophy of why there is a need for archaeology and gives insight into Joukowsky's own personal motivations and inspirations as an archaeologist. Fletcher and Bailey, on the other hand, look at the specific strengths of archaeology when

---

[7] Nelson, Sarah Milledge (ed). 2006. Archaeological Perspectives on Gender. In: Nelson, Sarah Milledge (ed). 2006. *Handbook of Gender in Archaeology*. AltaMira Press. USA. pp 9.

[8] White, Peter. 1974. *The Past is Human*. Angus and Robertson. Great Britain.

[9] Braidwood, Robert J. 1970. Quoted in: Cleator, P. E. 1976. *Archaeology in the Making*. St Martin's Press, New York.

[10] Ely, Talfourd. 1890. Quoted in: Cleator, P. E. 1976. *Archaeology in the Making*. St Martin's Press, New York.; Biek, Leo. 1963. Quoted in: Cleator, P. E. 1976. *Archaeology in the Making*. St Martin's Press, New York.

[11] Fagan, Brian M. 1978. *Archaeology – A Brief introduction*. Little, Brown and Co. Boston, Toronto. pp 2.

[12] Courbin, Paul. 1972. Quoted in: Cleator, P. E. 1976. *Archaeology in the Making*. St Martin's Press, New York.

[13] Crawford, O. G. S. 1953. Quoted in: Cleator, P. E. 1976. *Archaeology in the Making*. St Martin's Press, New York.

[14] Daniel, Glyn. 1950. *A hundred and fifty years of Archaeology*. Redwood Burn Ltd, Throwbridge and Esher. Great Britain. pp 9.

[15] Papanek, John (editor). 1992. *Egypt: Land of the Pharaohs*. Time Life Books, USA. pp 18-19.

[16] Chang, K. C. 1978. Some theoretical issues in the archaeological study of historical reality. In: Dunnell, Robert C. and Hall Jnr, Edwin S. (eds). 1978. *Archaeological essays in honour of Irving B. Rouse*. Mouton Publishers. The Hague, The Netherlands. pp 13.

[17] Movius, Hallam L. 1965. Quoted in: Cleator, P. E. 1976. *Archaeology in the Making*. St Martin's Press, New York.

[18] Bailey, G.N. 1983. Concepts of time in Quaternary prehistory. In: *Annual Review of Anthropology*. Volume 12: 165-192. Annual Reviews, USA. pp 165; Fletcher, Roland. 1986. Settlement Archaeology: world-wide comparisons. In: *World Archaeology*. Number 18 (1): 59-83.; Fletcher, Roland. 1995. *The Limits of Settlement Growth*. Cambridge University Press.

[19] Knudson, S. J. 1978. *Culture in Restrospect: An Introduction to Archaeology*. Rand and McNally College Publishing Company. Chicago. pp 4-5.

[20] Joukowsky, Martha. 1980. *Field Archaeology*. Prentice Hall Inc, New Jersey. pp 1.

defining their approaches, examining what archaeology can do that no other discipline can. Artifacts of great variety abound throughout the many environments of earth, some as large as 100 square kilometres, some as small as a fraction of a millimetre, some millions of years old, others as recent as yesterday. Fletcher and Bailey both point out that they form a consistent record of long-term human interaction with material, something that archaeology is uniquely positioned to effectively examine.[21] How that record is then used to reason about the past is a matter for ongoing debate and conjecture.

Unfortunately, the earliest arrivals were often more concerned with treasure than knowledge. Characters like Giovanni Battista Belzoni, an Italian strongman who liaised with tomb robbers in order to gain access to the valuables of the past buried throughout Egypt, were common. The majority of his experiences destroyed more than they illuminated, with him casually describing crushing sarcophagi in his stumbling rush through tombs, or even cooking roast chicken for dinner on a fire heated by fragments of broken sarcophagi, bones and other mummified remains.[22] Such misadventures were commonplace in a time period where excavation was more likely to be conducted by dynamite rather than brush and trowel. As a monument rather than a temple or tomb, the Great Sphinx of Giza remained relatively unscathed, but the occasional rumor that it housed a secret cache of treasure worked to its disadvantage, as per the drilling of holes in its body in 1838 by surveyor and engineer treasure-hunter John Shae Perring. It took time for scientific knowledge to presage treasure as the main motivation for study in Egypt, and even now tales of the treasure hunter era flavor contemporary understandings of archaeology and Egyptology.

[21] Fletcher, Roland. 1995. *The Limits of Settlement Growth*. Cambridge University Press. pp 188; Bailey, G.N. 1983. Concepts of time in Quaternary prehistory. In: *Annual Review of Anthropology*. Volume 12: 165-192. Annual Reviews, USA. pp 165.

[22] Belzoni, Giovanni Battista. 1820. *Narrative of the operations and recent discoveries within the pyramids, temples, tombs, and excavations, in Egypt and Nubia; and of a journey to the coast of the Red Sea, in search of the ancient Berenice, and of another to the oasis of Jupiter Ammon.* J. Murray, London.

A portrait of Giovanni Battista Belzoni

Although it is generally accepted in archaeology and Egyptology that Khafre was the pharaoh responsible for the construction of the Great Sphinx of Giza, there is still some ongoing debate about the matter. The evidence for Khafre consists of the proximity of his own pyramid to the monument, as well as the facial similarities of the Sphinx to other representations of Khafre from Egypt's archaeological record. The so-called dream stele of Thutmose IV has also been cited as referring to Khafre, but damage to the inscription means that this is also open to debate. It was archaeologist Thomas Young who noted Khaf written in hieroglyphs within a damaged cartouche, the design of which is usually utilized to denote a royal name, but by the time the stele was re-examined in 1925, the Khaf reference had been destroyed due to further flaking. Counter evidence to the Khafre hypothesis include another inscription, called the Inventory Stela, describing Khufu discovering the Sphinx already buried in sand during his era. This would mean that the Sphinx is even centuries older than previously thought, but the Inventory Stela dates to somewhere between 678 and 525 B.C., so the inscription has been interpreted as a revisionist story from the Late Period, making it an example of the propaganda of the past, with the ancient Egyptians rewriting their own already ancient history . Writer Colin Reader weighed the evidence and concluded "the execution of the Inventory Stela is poor and the names used for the various deities mentioned in the text are clearly those employed during the Late Period… [it is] a fraudulent attempt on the part of the Late Period Egyptians to re-discover a past which was, even then, of great antiquity."[23]

Archaeologist Rainer Stadelmann, who was once the director of the German Archaeological Institute in Cairo, stated the case against Khafre as the builder of the Sphinx through examination of the monument's iconography and surrounding architecture. Khafre's Causeway, he argued, was built around a pre-existing structure, with Stadelmann arguing based on location that the pre-existing structure was the Great Sphinx of Giza itself. Therefore, he reasoned, if the monument predated Khafre, its iconography would be indicative of an earlier period. Stadelmann argued this different iconography included the headdress or nemes of the Sphinx, as well as the one-time beard that has long since been detached from the monument along with its nose. The iconography of both beard and headdress, Stadelmann argued, were stylistically similar to the era of Pharaoh Khufu, reigning between 2589 and 2566 B.C.[24] As the builder of the Great Pyramid of Giza and father to Khafre, Khufu is a popular choice for alternate interpretations of the pharaoh who oversaw the creation of the Sphinx.

With that said, Stadelmann's argument of the causeway being built around an existing structure does not take into account the fact that the outcrop the Sphinx was carved from would have been a natural feature present in the landscape long before it was shaped into the likeness of the Sphinx. In other words, the causeway could have been constructed even before the Sphinx was finished, thereby making it possible that Khafre was responsible for both the Sphinx and the causeway. Despite the dissenting views, current consensus among Egyptologists is that Khafre was the pharaoh who instigated the sculpting of the Sphinx monument from a natural outcrop, left over following the completion of his father's Great Pyramid of Giza. Although this position may change if further evidence is acquired, it remains the most commonly accepted version of the past at this time.

The tomb was the most important part of the Egyptian mortuary complex. Indeed, ancient Egypt was a land full of tombs—which the ancient culture considered to be houses built for eternity. Accordingly, the tombs of Ancient Egypt had to be constructed with the most elaborate care and attention. Just as the Ancient Egyptian concept of eternity remained the same throughout the many centuries of the civilization's history, so too did the architectural components of tombs remain relatively constant. Each Egyptian tomb—regardless of its shape—contained a chapel, a passage or shaft to the burial chamber, and walls decorated with scenes of the daily life of the deceased. It was not uncommon for a pharaoh to pick out the location of his future tomb during the very first year of his reign, and at that point, the pharaoh would also begin to consider the tomb's architectural designs and the decorations by which the structure's walls and ceilings would be adorned.

The location a pharaoh selected for his tomb was of paramount importance, and the Valley of

[23] Reader, Colin. 2002. *Giza Before the Fourth Dynasty*. Journal of the Ancient Chronology Forum #9. pp 5–21. Site accessed 14 July 2013. http://www.thehallofmaat.com/modules.php?name=Articles&file=article&sid=93

[24] Stadelmann, Rainer. 2003. The Great Sphinx of Giza. In: Hawass, Zahi (editor). *Egyptology at the Dawn of the Twenty-First Century: Proceedings of the Eighth International Congress of Egyptologists*. American University in Cairo Press, Cairo and New York. pp. 464-469.

the Kings offered a great deal of suitable options. At its narrowest point, the Valley opens up, running to the west and the northwest until turning south to reveal its two main branches. The Valley of the Kings consists, in fact, of these two separate wadis (ravines). The first wadi is the main eastern branch of the Valley, and the second is the Valley's larger western branch.

The majority of the Valley's royal tombs are located in the eastern branch, which was known to the ancients as "ta set aat" (the Great Place) or sometimes simply as "ta int" (the Valley).[25] Within the eastern branch of the Valley are several smaller branches which are also littered with tombs.

The western branch of the Valley contains few known tombs. From the western branch, the wadi runs to the southwest through impressive, towering rock formations. The western branch of the wadi ends dramatically in a large natural amphitheater, which would have surely made it an appealing location for royal tombs had the "heretic king" Akhenaten not first chosen it as the location of his own tomb.

Indeed, it was Akhenaten's father, Amenhotep III, who first placed his tomb in the West Valley of the Kings, making him likely the first to utilize this more distant section of the royal necropolis. The tombs of the Western Valley were constructed partway up the slop of the talus slop at the end of a branch of the main wadi (valley). Many of the tombs in the Western Valley are unknown, but some seem to have belonged to the final members of the 18th dynasty. The tomb designated as KV 23, for example, was begun for Tutankhamun but was ultimately used for the internment of his successor Ay. The last pharaoh of the 18th dynasty, Horemheb, returned his tomb to the Eastern Valley, likely a move intended to symbolize his desire to restore Egypt's traditional rituals. As the 19th dynasty rose to power, they continued to cut their tomb entrances into the base of the talus slopes immediately above the wadi floor.

---

[25] Today the eastern branch is known as Biban el-Muluk (the Valley of the Doors of the Kings).

A picture of murals in KV 23, which Egyptologist John Wilkerson described as containing "a broken sarcophagus and some bad fresco painting of peculiarly short and graceless proportions"

In order to understand the pharaohs' original decisions for their tomb locations, it is important to understand the geology of the Theban West Bank. The Egyptologist Giovanni Belzoni, the first to describe the geology and topology of the Valley, noticed that the positioning of many tombs seemed to be based upon the Valley's drainage patterns, but more recent work on the Valley's geology has established that there are three groups of tombs which are related both hydrologically and geographically. These three tomb groupings appear to be closely related to the three Egyptian dynasties which used the Valley of the Kings as their royal necropolis.

The tombs of the early to mid-18th dynasty were typically quarried from the limestone clefts of the Valley's cliffs. Whenever possible, the pharaohs of the early 18th dynasty opted to construct their tombs beneath ancient waterfalls. After one of these pharaohs was buried in his tomb, the walls of the tomb's entrance were sealed over with stone and subsequently plastered shut. When floodwaters inevitably flooded the Valley later on, these tombs were buried—and thus hidden—beneath massive amounts of debris.

Later in the 18th dynasty and throughout much of the 19th, pharaohs usually opted to locate their tombs further down in the Valley at some distance from the rock walls. The builders often quarried through talus slopes in order to construct these tombs; accordingly, these tombs were far more susceptible to water damage than were their predecessors. Since some of these tombs made contact with the Valley's underlying layer of shale, they were also much more prone to damage from explosions. During the 20th dynasty, pharaohs preferred their tombs to be cut at ground level, often on the ends of rock spurs produced by the Valley's flood channels. This positioning offered at least some protection from floodwaters, but given the low-lying entrances of these tombs, water still tended to leak in.

The actual construction of these tombs was entrusted to an architect and the craftsmen who occupied the village of Deir el-Medina.[26] Every day, these workers would make the steep trek over the cliffs behind Deir al-Bahri (a commute of approximately 30 minutes) to the site of whatever tomb was currently under construction. It was the architect's job to direct the work of the craftsmen, who were typically divided into two groups: the left and the right. These groups did not have a set number of workmen; usually, they consisted of between 30-60 workmen, but there were times when each group could contain as many as 120 workers. Though working days varied, these workmen typically worked 8 hour days beginning at dawn. The work week lasted for 10 days, after which the laborers were given only two days to rest. Workers also received many additional days off for both religious festivals and personal leave.

These laborers were usually highly specialized, including stone-cutters, plasterers, draftsmen, and artists responsible for decorating the tomb's surfaces. The left team and the right team typically worked in their respective parts of the tomb under the direct supervision and control of two foremen, one for each team, and these foremen were often appointed by either the pharaoh himself or the pharaoh's vizier. It was the responsibility of the tomb's foremen both to partake in the work itself and to deal with the pharaoh's vizier and the vizier's scribe, who was tasked with providing the workers with food (which constituted their wages) from the pharaoh's warehouses, settling any quarrels that might arise among the workers, and generally administering justice in the village of Deir el-Medina.

Work on a tomb resembled working on an assembly line. First, the quarrymen would come to dig the tomb into the mountain. Next, the plasterers would come to smooth the walls of the new tomb using a type of plaster called *muna*, which was made from limestone, quartz, clay, and crushed straw. Over this layer of *muna*, the plasterers placed thin layers of limestone and clay, which they whitened with a final layer of diluted gypsum. Once the tomb was sufficiently plastered, the draftsmen would come to execute the design which had been decided upon by Egypt's high priests and approved by the pharaoh himself. These draftsmen utilized red ochre to divide the walls and surfaces of the new tomb so the figures and texts of the tomb's decorations could be placed exactly where they belonged. A chief draftsman oversaw this work, and once a "first draft" was complete, the overseeing draftsman would inspect the divisions and make corrections using black charcoal. Once these divisions were finalized, it was time for the

---

[26] The workmen's village at Deir el Medina is one of the most thoroughly documented communities of the ancient world. Located about a half mile beyond the cultivated land which bordered the Nile River—between the Valley of the Kings and the Valley of the Queens. The settlement was formed at some point during the 18th dynasty, most likely during the reign of Thutmose I, who was the first pharaoh to be buried in the Valley of the Kings.

sculptors to come in and begin carving the bas-relief. After the bas-relief was carved, painters came to color it. These painters employed six basic colors, each of which was ritually symbolic.[27]

Several other kinds of workers were also employed in tomb construction. The unskilled sons of skilled craftsmen were often employed in more menial tasks, and each skilled craftsmen was provided with a team of common laborers who performed minor tasks such as keeping torches burning,[28] carrying water, and preparing plaster. Thus, even as the craftsmen worked in the deepest sections of the tombs near the entrance, work always continued efficiently. Even though these craftsmen had access to only the most rudimentary tools, it typically took them no more than a few months to complete an average tomb. The larger, more elaborate tombs could take from between 6-10 years to complete.

Peter Bubenik's picture of the area around the entrance to KV 62

These royal tombs which were cut into the Valley of the Kings represented a shift in both form

---

[27] Green (wadj) was the color of vegetation and new life; red (desher) was the color of life and victory; white (hedj and shesep) was the color of omnipotence and purity; black (kem) was the color that symbolized death and night; yellow (khenet) was the color of the sun and gold, thus, the symbol of the imperishable, eternal, and indestructible; blue (iritu and sbedj) symbolized both water and sky, thus, the symbol of the heavens, the primeval flood, and fertility.

[28] These were specialized torches. Baked clay containers were filled with salt and sesame oil or animal fat. The salt helped to limit the amount of smoke emitted by the torch in order to ensure that none of the paintings in the tomb would be harmed.

and location from the pyramid complexes preceding them. Though the tombs in the Valley vary in detail, they all took on the essential form of a hollowed out chamber deep inside the cliffs. Some tombs in the Valley of the King were cut as much as 500 feet deep into the hillside. The entrances of these tombs were always carefully concealed in an admirable (but almost always hopeless) attempt to prevent the tombs of the Valley from being plundered by tomb robbers. In fact, some papyrus scrolls describe the exploits of the robbers, including one written by an individual who robbed the tomb of Ramesses VI: "The foreigner Nesamun took us up and showed us the tomb of King Ramesses VI ... And I spent four days breaking into it, we being present all five. We opened the tomb and entered it. ... We found a cauldron of bronze, three wash bowls of bronze ..."

Though each tomb in the Valley was unique, each was designed using the same basic components. First was the tomb's entranceway, which was a stairway, a ramp, or a shaft that was cut into the rock of the hillside or cliff face. In the 18th dynasty, tomb entranceways tended to take the form of a steep stairway, and this trend continued until the later part of the 19th dynasty, when the slope of the staircase decreased substantially. By the time of the 20th dynasty, the opening of the entryway had become much larger and the slope of the descending staircase had become quite shallow. The entry cuttings of 20th dynasty tombs were occasionally augmented on the sides of their top and front ends by rubble walls, though in some of the simpler tombs, the entryway was nothing more than a vertical shaft.

The entryway of a tomb led to several corridors, and the number of corridors in a tomb was dependent on the date of the tomb's construction and the amount of time builders were given to complete the tomb. Most commonly, there were three chambers between the entranceway and what was known as the well chamber, and one or two more between a larger pillared chamber and the chamber by which the burial chamber itself was preceded. The floors and ceilings of these corridors were generally parallel and flat, and the sides of their walls were almost always straight.

Over time, the width and height of these corridors tended to increase while the slope of their floors and ceilings tended to decrease. By the late 20th dynasty, the floors and ceilings of tomb corridors were hardly sloped at all. If there were any gates in the tomb, the sloping ceilings of the tombs featured recesses so that these gates could be opened and closed.

Other specialized recessed were cut in pairs in the walls of these corridors. One recess was square, and the other was rectangular. The end of a rectangular beam was inserted into the square recess while the other end swung in an arc into the rectangular recess. Ropes were passed around these beams and attached to the sarcophagus. Once these ropes were (carefully) released, the sarcophagus was able to safely descend to the horizontal surface at the bottom of the burial chamber.

About half of the tombs in the Valley contained a chamber called the well chamber. The well chamber contained a deep well shaft, sometimes with a side chamber off the bottom of the shaft. Some scholars speculate that this shaft was intended to deter tomb robbers, while others claim that it existed to collect any floodwater that might have entered the tomb. A third theory suggests that the shaft in this chamber represented the burial place of the Memphite necropolis god Sokar, who was identified with Osiris. During the Rameside period, the decorations on the wall of the chamber immediately preceding the well chamber depicted the fourth and fifth hours of the Imydwat, the hours during which the sun god Ra passed over the burial place of Sokar. The walls of the chamber in which the shaft was cut were typically decorated with scenes of the pharaoh in the presence of various deities, especially Hathor, Isis, Horus, Osiris, and Anubis.

The pillared chamber was the location that allowed for the tomb to change from one axial orientation to another. During the 18th dynasty, this chamber consisted of only two pillars, and the stepped descent in its floor was set to one of its sides. It has been proposed that one purpose of this chamber was to provide enough space to safely maneuver the sarcophagus into the burial chamber. Later on, the sarcophagus descended into the center of the chamber, which by that point had begun to feature four chambers. If a tomb contained side chambers, they were most likely located off the pillared chamber. Usually, these side chambers were intended to hold food offerings and other funerary equipment.

The last chamber—the burial chamber—was by far the most important part of the tomb. Beginning with the tomb of Thutmose III, New Kingdom burial chambers were decorated with almost no exception. At the rear of the chamber, beyond a set of pillars, the royal sarcophagus lay in a sunken part of the chamber. During the late 18th dynasty, the sunken area featured a vaulted ceiling above it and was located in the center of the burial chamber. Almost every burial chamber was accessed by a stepped or ramped descent which was cut from the entrance of the tomb to the sunken area of the sarcophagus. Two sets of four columns on the main floor of the burial chamber flanked this sunken level. The upper edges of the sunken level seem to have been carved as cavetto cornices, and their vertical faces were usually decorated with images of burial equipment.

Murals in Thutmose III's tomb

The entrance to Thutmose III's tomb

The sarcophagus was often placed on some sort of structure or excavation which was set into the sunken part of the burial chamber's floor. In many instances, a base of high-quality limestone or Egyptian alabaster provided a base for the sarcophagus. This was placed in a recess or several recesses cut into the burial chamber's floor. In a few other instances, the sarcophagus was placed directly into a depression cut into the chamber's floor. Occasionally, the body—with or without a coffin—was placed into a pit cut into the floor of the burial chamber. This pit was then covered with stone slabs or a single stone covering and was a substitute for the freestanding box and lid of which a true sarcophagus was comprised.

At first, the mummified remains of elite Egyptians were enclosed within a nested set of coffins,[29] which were then placed in a sarcophagus. The sarcophagus was usually a stone box covered with a lid. A line of hieroglyphics ran vertically down the back of the sarcophagus to represent the backbone of the deceased, and these were also thought to provide strength to the mummy whenever he rose to eat or drink.

In the Valley of the Kings, most of the deceased were buried in cartouche-shaped sarcophagi. During the early New Kingdom period, these sarcophagi were made of stone, but later, they were carved from quartzite (a metamorphic form of sandstone). Towards the end of the 18th dynasty, the sarcophagi found in the Theban necropolis utilized red Aswan granite. The sarcophagi of the 18th dynasty pharaohs were usually decorated with representations of Anubis and the four sons of Horus on the sides, while the foot and head ends depicted Isis and Nephthys. Towards the end of the dynasty, the sarcophagi came to be rectangular, with sculpted figures of protective goddesses decorating their corners.

---

[29] These were all mummiform. Their decorations often included a rishi (feather) pattern. Royal sarcophagi included the striped nemes headdress with a ureaeus on the brow and the "crook and flail" scepters in the hand. Occasionally coffins, like sarcophagi, were also set one inside the other.

Pictures of Tutankhamun's mummy and sarcophagus

With the tomb of Ramesses I, the founder of Egypt's 19th dynasty, there was a return to the cartouche-shaped sarcophagus; though different royal buries utilized different forms of sarcophagi. Seti I and Ramesses II were interred in Egyptian alabaster mummiform sarcophagi, and these were inscribed with scenes and texts taken from the Imydwat and the Book of Gates. Merenptah was buried in an especially impressive sarcophagus which managed to combine the shrine shape of past sarcophagi with the cartouche shape of the neo-modern sarcophagus. A mummiform effigy was featured on two of these sarcophagus' lids, and again, these were decorated with extracts taken from the Imdyway and the Book of Gates. Every pharaoh of the 19th dynasty through the reign of Ramesses IV would be buried in such an elaborate sarcophagus.

The sarcophagus of Merenptah

With the burial of Siptah, the form and decorative program of the royal sarcophagi became more standardized. The cartouche shape was used consistently, and the effigy on each lid was accompanied by the figures of Isis and Nephthys. A serpent sat to the left of the king, with a crocodile to his right. The exteriors of these late 19th dynasty sarcophagi featured experts from the Book of the Earth.

Certain internal organs, including the liver, lungs, stomach, and intestines, were removed from the body of the deceased and mummified separately, so they required containers outside of the coffin. These containers were called canopic jars. Both the four separately mummified internal organs and their canopic containers were believed to be under the protection of the Four Sons of Horus, and each Son was responsible for a specific organ.[30] The tombs of the New Kingdom Pharaohs in the Valley of the Kings thus featured a stone, shrine-shaped box which featured four compartments. This was known as a canopic chest, and it was typically made of the same material as the royal sarcophagus (quartzite for Hatshepsut, Thutmose I, and Thutmose III; calcite for Amenhotep II and those by whom he was succeeded).

The canopic chest of Amenhotep II introduced a new decorative program. Figures of the four protective goddesses—Isis, Nephthys, Neit, and Serquet—were sculpted on the corners with their arms extended so that they seemed to embrace the sides of the chest. The chest's individual

---

[30] Imset protected the liver, Hapy the lungs, Duamutef the stomach, and Qebehsenuf the intestines.

compartments were closed by stoppers fashioned in the shape of the respective pharaoh's head. Each mummified organ was wrapped separately, and occasionally, it was provided with its own miniature mummy mask or even its own coffin. The canopic chest was most likely placed at the foot of the sarcophagus, though it may have sometimes been located in a separate side chamber located off the main burial chamber.

A set of Ancient Egyptian canopic jars made during the 21st dynasty

Shabti were mummiform statuettes that served as substitutes for deceased when the deceased were called to go perform tasks in the realm of Osiris. Each shabti was inscribed with the name of its owner, and, usually, with Spell 6[31] of the Book of the Dead. Shabti could be fashioned out of a number of different materials, including faience, stone (granite, sandstone, limestone, quartzite, or alabaster), and wood. Some were made of bronze, while a few were made of wood and subsequently gilded with silver or gold leaf. Most wood shabti, however, were simply coated with black resin.

---

[31] "O shabti, allotted to me, if I be summoned or if I be detailed to do any work which has to be done in the realm of the dead, if indeed any obstacles are implanted for you therewith as a man at his duties, you shall detail yourself for me on every occasion of making arable the fields, of flooding the banks or of conveying sand from east to west; 'Here I am', you shall say."

A picture of several shabti

Pictures of shabti of Tutankhamun

Most shabti were found with their own separate set of miniature tools—mattocks and baskets—that they would need complete their tasks. In theory, each shabti would have required one worker for each workday, an overseer for every 10 days, and a higher ranking overseer for each month, as well as five additional workers for the five epagomenal days that occurred at the end of an Egyptian year. In other words, they needed 413 in total. The more shabti dolls present in a tomb, the greater the wealth of the person who was buried there.[32]

---

[32] Each shabti could only use once as a replacement, so the demand for them was extremely high. An entire

Royal tombs were always filled with a number of wooden figures of the king, various deities, and protective creatures. Sometimes, these figures were even enclosed in their own individual, miniature shrines. One of the most common ritual figures was a hollowed tray or box made in the shape of the god Osiris. This box was called a germinating Osiris, as it was filled with seeded dirt. Whenever the dirt was moistened, the seeds of the germinating Osiris would sprout.

Also common was a specialized group of ritual figures which were attached to magical bricks. These figures, which always came in a set of four, were oriented to the cardinal directions and placed in niches carved into the four walls of the burial chamber so that they surrounded the coffin. Each of these mud bricks was inscribed with protective texts from Spell 151 of the Book of the Dead. Almost every tomb also contained a number of models, most commonly a model of a boat. These model boats served a number of functions, including sailing to and from Abydos on the deceased's ritual pilgrimage to the tomb of Osiris and generally traversing the murky waters of the realms of Osiris.

From as early as the 5th dynasty, it had become traditional for religious texts to be inscribed in the burial chambers of royal tombs. The oldest of these surviving compositions were called the Pyramid Texts, as they were inscribed in the burial chambers of the Great Pyramids. Generally, these texts were a compilation of spells which described different aspects of the pharaoh's restoration and his existence among the gods in the afterlife.

A picture of Pyramid Texts in Teti I's pyramid

industry was devoted to their creation.

During the Middle Kingdom period, rulers ceased this practice and instead preferred to have a series of spells depicted on their coffins. These were called Coffin Texts, though most were derived directly from the Pyramid Texts. More innovatively, however, the floors of Middle Kingdom coffins offered some of the first depictions of the afterlife in the form of a schematic map, and this map and accompanying text came to be known as "The Book of Two Ways." New Kingdom funerary compositions consisted of elements from both the Old and Middle Kingdom traditions.

The vast majority of the funerary compositions found in the Valley of the Kings featured both figures and texts that described the afterlife in the Field of Reeds. The Book of Caverns, so named because its figures are shown in ovals which are meant to represent caves, is divided into just six sections. Amun-Ra in the form of a ram-headed man introduces the first four divisions, and the lower registers of the first five divisions contain depictions of bound enemies. In the fifth division are depicted two large figures of Nut and ithyphallic Osiris. In the sixth division, the concluding scene, the sun god Amun-Ra dawns as a scarab and a child as he emerges from the watery realm of creation.

A scene from the fifth division of the Book of Caverns

Another popular scene was known as the Book of the Earth. Unlike most descriptions of the solar nightly journey, the Book of the Earth does not follow an obvious narrative progression. Instead, three registers on the left wall of the tomb depict the sun god Amun-Ra in his sacred bark (barge) beneath a supine mummy. Star and sun disks shine over both figures. The bottom register depicts an ithyphallic figure in a structure which was meant to resemble a water clock On the right wall of the tomb was the "*ba*" form of Amun-Ra—a large, ram-headed bird which lies beneath a representation of the reborn sun as it emerges from the waters of chaos. Beneath the outstretched wings of Amun-Ra's *ba*, the bark of the sun god rests on the image of Aker, the dual-headed sphinx. Aker represented the embodied form of the earthly entrance to the underworld. A goddess representing the Hours was shown facing the sun god Amun-Ra.

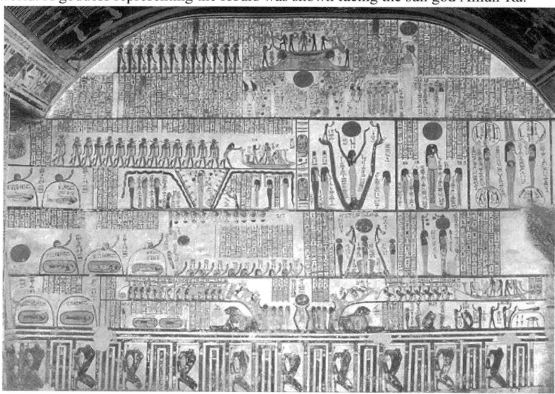

The Book of the Earth in KV 9

The tomb and calcite sarcophagus of the pharaoh Seti I features one of the only complete versions of the Book of Gates,[33] though certain sections of the Book appeared with some frequency in a great number of other tombs. Each section of the Book of Gates (except for the last) was divided into three registers. The first registers depicted the solar boat as it enters the western horizon; the sun god and his barge appear in the beginning of the middle register. The fifth register was enlarged and depicted the Judgment Hall of Osiris. In the closing scene, the god Nun was seen raising the sacred bark from the primeval waters at dawn. It was also popular for the vaulted ceilings of burial chambers to be decorated with figures that represented the constellations of both the northern and southern horizons. Other figures on the ceilings represented the decans, the starts which were used to herald the three 10 day long intervals into which every month was divided. Complementing these astronomical figures on the ceilings were often scenes from the Books of the Day and Night, in which the arched figure of Nut, the sky goddess, frames texts which describe the sun god Amun Ra's journey across the sky as he proceeds from sunrise to sunset, as well as his nightly journey within her body—beginning with her swallowing him—until his eventual rebirth at dawn.

---

[33] The only other complete version exists on the south walls of the upper corridors and chambers of the tomb of Ramses V and VI.

A picture of the ceiling in Seti I's burial chamber

Still other compositions which (partially or completely) adorned the royal tombs of the Valley of the Kings included the Book of the Heavenly Cow, which describes how Amun-Ra's daughter Hathor averted the destruction of mankind. Its principle image featured a large cow supported by the image of the god Shu. Complete versions of this composition were found inside the outmost gilded shrine of King Tutankhamun, as well as in a side chamber of the tomb of Seti I. The burial chamber of Ramses IV features a composition called the Book of Nut, in which Shu, the god of the air, is depicted supporting the arched figure of the sky goddess Nut, and thus he separates her from Geb, the god of the earth.

A depiction of the Book of the Heavenly Cow

Later in the 20th dynasty, royal tombs also began to feature star clocks. The measurement of time using celestial phenomenon had always played an important role in funerary text and tomb decoration, and in later tombs, this tradition was celebrated with depictions of men kneeling beneath grids which contained stars. Besides each kneeling man was the name of the star that appeared on a particular point on the human target at a given hour of the night, essential a sun-dial which utilized other stars. One image and one name were usually given to mark each month of the year.

Amun-Ra's journey through the underworld was the vastly predominant theme of most funeral compositions, but many royal tombs also featured compositions of a non-royal nature. Most royal tombs contained at least a few spells from the Book of the Dead, which dealt with the solar journey, the final judgment, the portals of the realm of Osiris, and various descriptions of the underworld. Spells from the Book of the Dead were commonly found on the sarcophagi of the pharaohs of the 18th dynasty, but by the time King Tutankhamun was buried, they had begun to appeal on the burial chamber walls as well.

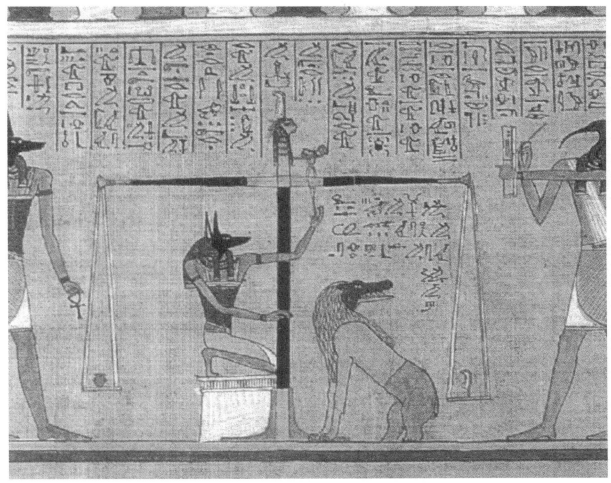
A scene from the Book of the Dead

Of near equal popularity was the Litany of Re. The initial scene of the Litany depicts the sun disk with a crocodile below it and a serpent above it. Inside the disk are a scarab (the sun god at sunrise) and a ram-headed man (the sun god at noon). Following these images, the sun god was invoked in seventy-four forms, with each form followed by its image. On the ceiling of the chamber that depicted the Litany, the ceiling offered still another representation of the sun god as a ram-headed bird (his "*ba*" form) accompanied by Isis and Nephthys in the form of kites.

Finally, many royal tombs contained at least some portion of the scenes from the Opening of the Mouth ritual. This text consisted of a number of spells which were concerned with restoring the body of the deceased back to life, as well as with the animation of a statue or image with spiritual force. These spells were always accompanied by images of priests who were performing them before either the deceased himself or a statue of the deceased.

Memphis and the Great Pyramids

Since excavating the actual city of Memphis has proven excessively difficult, the vast majority of information about the golden age of Memphis comes from excavations of its nearby royal necropolises. As it turns out, the way in which the rulers of Old Kingdom Memphis prepared for their deaths provides an abundance of information about what was going on while they lived.

This is, of course, a frustratingly indirect way of piecing together the history of the great city, but there can be no doubt that the rich archaeological legacy discovered at the sites of the Memphite necropolises provides at least some consolation for the near-silent record of "living" Memphis.

As such, some of the best evidence for Memphis' rise to preeminence comes from the royal tombs which were first built at Saqqara by the pharaohs of the second dynasty. It is at Saqqara, for example, that archaeologists have discovered two suites of subterranean rock-cut chambers and galleries, which they have associated with the pharaohs Hotepsekhemwi and Nynetjer. Each of these subterranean suites had an astonishing storage capacity (4,000 square meters in the case of Hotepsekhemwi) in order to ensure that the tomb could hold the full wealth of the deceased pharaoh. These second dynasty tombs were significantly more intricate than their first dynasty counterparts, which had consisted of little more than a series of pits dug into the ground. In contrast, the tombs of the second dynasty pharaohs were comprised of long, subterranean corridors with plenty of storage rooms on either side to ensure that the pharaoh interred within would not be without any of his wealth and treasure in the afterlife.

Pictures of inscriptions and art found in pharaohs' tombs in Saqqara

By the third dynasty (the last dynasty of the Early Dynastic Period), Memphis had unquestionably become the greatest city in Ancient Egypt. Mantheo calls the third and fourth dynasties the first truly Memphite dynasty, a fact which may be confirmed by the huge royal pyramids that were first built at Saqqarah during this period. As the royal government had at last managed to reestablish a somewhat firm central authority over the entirety of Egypt, the pharaohs of the third dynasty were free to turn their attention towards less immediate concerns, such as architectural achievement.

Djoser (~2670-2640 B.C.E), the first pharaoh of the third dynasty, was the first pharaoh to attempt the construction of a stone pyramid, the form that would continue to influence the shape of Egyptian buildings for millennia to come. The implications of Djoser's step pyramid cannot be overstated. The structure is inextricably linked to the history and culture of the ancient city of Memphis and indeed all of Ancient Egypt, and it is perhaps one of the single most ambitious and revolutionary building projects ever completed.

The Step Pyramid, also known as the Pyramid of Djoser

**A relief inside the tomb of the Step Pyramid depicts Djoser facing the temple of Horus.
Photo by Juan R. Lazaro**

The tradition of pyramid building was a long one in ancient Egypt occurring over hundreds of years, with techniques developing and improving only to be forgotten and lost again. As a result, even as subsequent generations contributed new large-scale construction programs that changed the face of Egypt, they did so in quite different manners. That said, Djoser's was the first. In Egyptian times, it was referred to as kbhw-ntrw, and though it was commissioned by and made for the burial of Djoser, its design and construction was overseen by his vizier Imhotep. The name Imhotep has since become infused with popular culture through the popular series of Mummy movies, where the mummified remains of Imhotep are reanimated through the power of an ancient curse, leading to the shambling, linen-wrapped and decomposing undead monster haunting the hapless treasure seekers who dared disturb his resting place. In reality, the ancient Imhotep was a talented architect and builder who succeeded in creating something that had never been seen before.

The construction of Djoser's step-pyramid complex was motivated by the same political concerns that had preoccupied his predecessors. In order to secure the still fragile peace of the newly unified nation, Djoser realized that he needed to direct the nation's attention to a symbol of the centralized authority of his divine kingship. The best way to do this, he thought, was through the construction of his monumental tomb. Though previous pharaohs had left behind impressive legacies in the form of royal tombs, these tombs had been made of mudbrick and were not completed until after the pharaoh in question had died. Moreover, most of the tombs of Djoser's predecessors had also been ruined during the civil wars that had befallen Egypt in the two centuries following its original unification by Menes. Djoser therefore wanted to build something more permanent, as a symbol of the new, united order. Accordingly, he wanted everything in his tomb to be constructed from stone—even the elements like window frames and doors that would usually be constructed from wood. On an equally symbolic level, Djoser's immense project required material resources from all over the kingdom, as well as the work of thousands of laborers hailing from all parts of Egypt.

In building the pyramid. Imhotep almost singlehandedly developed a tradition of stone masonry. Previously, tomb construction involved little more than shoveling mud into wooden forms, but for the tomb that Djoser envisioned, however, stones had to be precisely cut and dressed into standard sizes, which could only be done by skilled laborers. Though Egypt had a few stone carvers who knew how to make cosmetic pallets, stone bowls, and other small items, these were relatively few in number and the scale of the tomb Djoser wanted would have vastly exceeded anything they could have conceived. Thus, Imhotep would have needed to have trained them and hundreds of other laborers from all over Egypt in the art of monumental stone-cutting.

Imhotep also needed to find laborers who could quarry and transport the stone needed for Djoser's tomb. Though most of the stone could be found at the site of the project, the outer casing of the pyramid required fine limestone that could only be brought from the quarries at Tura, which was located on the opposite side of the Nile River. Both those who carved the stone and those who quarried the stone required food and housing, meaning that Imhotep must have also overseen whole fleets of brewers, butchers, and bakers.

Such was the labor force necessary to complete the immense Djoser complex. By the time of its completion, the Djoser complex covered an impressive 15 hectares, and its dominant element, the step pyramid, stood nearly 200 feet above the plain. Upon its completion, Djoser's step pyramid was the tallest structure in Egypt and may well have been the tallest structure in the entire world. In addition to the massive pyramid, the Djoser complex consisted of two large courtyards, as well as a number of shrines, temples, and other buildings. The entire complex was surrounded by a limestone enclosure wall which itself measured well over 10 meters tall.

Construction of the step pyramid itself took place over several stages. Djoser had originally planned to build a traditional mastaba, but he intended this mastaba to be square instead of rectangular and fashioned of stone instead of wood. Thus, the base of the step pyramid measured approximately 64 square meters and measured approximately 8 meters in height. Its core consisted of irregular stone blocks which were packed with a local clay called tafla. This core was covered with a sloping outer dressing which was made from Tura limestone. Given that the structure's square shape was unprecedented in Ancient Egypt, some Egyptologists have proposed that Djoser always intended his tomb to be a stepped structure, but one which was built on a significantly smaller scale than the scale of the actual final structure. The fact that the original "mastaba" was almost immediately expanded three meters in all directions except its height supports this interpretation of the structure.

Before long, the "mastaba" was extended 10 meters to the east so that its superstructure adequately covered all the openings of its subterranean galleries. At this point, Djoser's structure measured 70 x 80 meters and may or may not have been finished as it was originally designed. Mastabas had, after all, been the traditional form of Egyptian tombs up to this point; however, it was not unprecedented for these mastabas to contain a stepped mound within a larger, rectangular superstructure. Furthermore, it is unclear why Djoser would have chosen to build his tomb as a stepped pyramid. Some scholars have suggested that the steps were meant to represent a stairway to the immortal stars; others that it was intended to be a representation of the primeval Mound of Creation. Still others suspect that its stepped structure was purely practical—perhaps with any other design, the Egyptians could not have built such a tall structure without it being liable to collapse.

Shortly after the construction of the pyramid's mastaba base was complete, Imhotep set about erecting a step-pyramid that, as he originally intended, would rise to 40 meters over four stages; however, this was soon enlarged to a 60 meter pyramid over six stages. For this, somewhat ironically given Djoser's original desire for an unprecedentedly square tomb, Imhotep ended up resting these stages on a rectangular base that measured 125 x 110 meters. Every other Egyptian pyramid would be built upon a square base.

As a revolutionary building project, the scope of Djoser's pyramid complex borders on the inconceivable. Constructing the additional five stages of the structure, required an astonishing 850,000 (more) tons of stone! Each course of stone was laid in a series of buttresses so that it was inclined inwards at a 75 degree angle. Thus, the amount of lateral stress was reduced, guaranteeing the stability of the immense final structure. The core of the pyramid's structure was built of small blocks of limestone. These limestone blocks were subsequently encased in fine, white Tura limestone. The entire pyramid complex was, at the time of its construction, surrounded by a giant trench that the workmen had cut into the surrounding bedrock. There can be little doubt that the stone taken from this trench was utilized in the construction of the core pyramid structure; however, archaeologists have also discovered that the workmen carved niches into the inner façade of the trench. If the trench was used only as a quarry, these niches would have served no purpose whatsoever. Some Egyptologists therefore speculate that these niches were built so that the spirits of the royal retainers could come out and serve Djoser once they had joined him in the afterlife—a less violent reimagining of the first dynasty tradition in which servants of the pharaoh were buried alive in the tomb of their master. It is highly possible, therefore, that these niches were meant to serve as still another reminder of the eternal and unchanging nature of the pharaoh's authority.

Below the superstructure of Djoser's step pyramid was a burial chamber which was accessed through square vertical shaft which extended 28 meters below the earth. As they quarried the site, the workmen had begun to dig a sloping corridor which they at first intended to be a trench—as they dug deeper, this trench became a tunnel. This tunnel served a dual purpose. While the workmen were building the pyramid, they used it to carry any rubble away. Once the pyramid was complete, the tunnel became an entrance passage.

At the bottom of this long vertical shaft was Djoser's burial chamber. This burial chamber was a modest, oblong room formed out of slabs of pink granite. Archaeologists have discovered evidence of an earlier vault, the walls of which were constructed of alabaster and paved with either schist or diorite. Broken fragments of this earlier vault were used as packing material around the final burial chamber. Among the debris believed to have belonged to this early vault, archaeologists have found a number of fragments which were decorated with five pointed stars— these, it is believed, formed the ceiling of the original vault. A small hole was left in the ceiling of the final burial chamber; it was through this hole that Djoser's body was admitted for his final interment. The hole was so small that it would have been impossible to fit a sarcophagus through it. After the last funeral rite had been performed for Djoser, this hole was sealed with a 3.5 ton granite plug.

Somewhat puzzlingly, the opposite (southern) side of the Djoser complex housed another "secondary" tomb inside a long, rectangular building with a low, vaulted roof. Djoser's secondary tomb was composed of more or less the same elements as his pyramid tomb, though its structure varied slightly from that of the primary tomb. Secondary tombs were apparently somewhat common among Old Kingdom pyramid complexes; however, they were by no means found at every pyramid. Some have speculated that secondary tombs such as the one found at the Djoser pyramid complex were used to inter the pharaoh's principle wives, but the size of the South Tomb precludes this possibility, as it was far too small to hold the remains of an adult woman and her coffin. Thus, there are some who speculate that the Djoser pyramid complex was built to house Djoser's mummified internal organs (specifically, his stomach, lungs, liver, and intestines) or his royal placenta, which had been preserved since his birth. The majority of Egyptologists believe that secondary temples were built as tombs for the deceased pharaoh's ka, which would have lay therein in the form of a statue.

Like Djoser's primary tomb, the secondary tomb was accessed through a descending corridor. Approximately halfway down this corridor was found a rectangular galley that had been filled with an assortment of stone jars and pottery. On top of these vessels lay a wooden box, a wooden stretcher, and a set of canopy polls that still bear the traces of the gold leaf with which they were embellished. It has been suggested that this stretcher was used to carry these vessels into the tomb and discarded there when it was no longer needed; however, it seems far more plausible that this stretcher was used for the transportation of a royal statue—perhaps even Djoser's ka statue.

Like the main pyramid tomb, the secondary tomb contained a number of galleries which were decorated with radiant faience in an imitation of the reed mat panels and doorways of the pharaoh's private apartments within the royal palace. Djoser's Horus name, Netjerykhet, and his many titles were inscribed upon the door jambs and lintels of each gallery. The reliefs in the secondary tomb were thematically the same as the reliefs of the main tomb—within them, Djoser was seen as he took part in a number of rituals. He sports a false beard and the crown of Upper Egypt while donning (at most) the crown of Upper Egypt. In his right hand, he wields a flail—an agricultural threshing tool and potent symbol of the pharaoh's power. In his right hand he holds an unknown fishtailed object that archaeologists believe was used by priests in the Opening of the Mouth ceremony to reanimate the bodies of the deceased. Standing guard over his head is Horus, the god of kingship, holding the ankh (life) symbol in his talons. At his front is a standard which depicts a jackal, Wepwawet, who is seen dancing between the two horse-shoe shaped markers of the Heb-Sed ritual.

Surrounding Djoser's main burial chamber were a number of other corridors, each of which led to a number of galleries. Most of these galleries functioned as storage magazines; however, a few of the galleries along the eastern side of the complex seem to have been replications of the pharaoh's own private apartments as they had existed in the royal palace at Memphis. The outmost of the palace-like galleries had western walls that featured panels of inlaid faience tiles; these imitated the actual reed matting of the Memphite palace. The intricacy of these tiles was nothing short of incredible—each had a back with a tendon so that it could be carefully fitted into a mortice that had been draughted for it with equal care. Even the colors of the tiles' faience was symbolic—only blue and green, the colors associated with regeneration and rebirth, were utilized on these walls. Moreover, each panel featured a number of djed-pillers as they stood supporting an arch. This was a powerful (and permanent) symbol of stability. Between each panel stood reliefs of Djoser as he performed a number of restorative religious ceremonies, including the important Heb-Sed ritual. That these ceremonies were depicted on the walls of his tomb mean that Djoser's ka would perform these rites for all eternity in the afterlife.

Along the tomb's eastern side were 11 other vertical shafts, each of which reached a depth of 32 meters. At the bottom of each of these 11 chambers was a lengthy gallery that extended for several meters below the pyramid's superstructure. Archaeologists believe that each of these chambers was intended to serve as a burial chamber for a member of the royal family, as one contained an empty alabaster sarcophagus and a coffin which held the remains of a young boy. Fragments of two other sarcophagi have been found in the first two galleries. Many of the other galleries were filled to the brim with all kinds of stone vessels (over 40,000 in total!). As many of these vessels were engraved with the names of first and second dynasty pharaohs, some have speculated that they were looted from earlier tombs, though many believe that they were collected by Djoser himself in order to protect them from the factional strife that had caused so much destruction during the second dynasty.

At the northern side of the pyramid complex was Djoser's mortuary temple—a collection of rooms, corridors, and open courtyards that contained shrines meant to hold offerings for the deceased pharaoh; seemingly, the courtyards which housed these shrines were intended to represent Upper and Lower Egypt. Behind the mortuary temple, built up against the northern side of the step pyramid, was a small, separate enclosure. This enclosure, which could only be entered through its (permanently opened) stone gates, contained a courtyard with a tiny, sealed serab (cellar) at its rear. Inside this serab was a exquisitely painted limestone statue of the enthroned

Djoser wearing a long Heb-Sed robe that covers his entire body, from his ankles all the way to his shoulders. Within the sealed serab, as the Ancient Egyptians believed, the ka of the Djoser could, using the eyes of his image, come to view any sacrifices and rites that were performed in his honor; thus, the builders took care to pierce the outer wall of the serab with two eye-level holes.

Djoser's step-pyramid was designed to be the central element within a larger "pyramid complex." This complex was surrounded by a 10 meter high enclosure wall. Like the galleries near Djoser's burial chamber, this limestone enclosure wall was meant to emulate the towering white walls of the royal palace—its façade was patterned upon the characteristic niches and buttresses of the palace enclosure wall. This was a relatively common pattern for enclosure walls—it was found in Abydos on the funerary enclosures of several pharaohs, as well as at Saqqara on several contemporaneous mastabas. In fact, the workmen must have been so accustomed to carving niches into mudbrick after it was already laid that they attempted to use the same technique on the stone of Djoser's enclosure wall. The wall contained no less than fifteen separate "gateways," each of which was guarded by a massive tower; however, fourteen of these gateways were false. According to the Ancient Egyptians, the spirits of the dead used these false gateways to come receive any offerings their descendants may have left for them.

The main—indeed the only—entrance to the Djoser pyramid complex was located at the southeast corner. The actual gateway could be distinguished from the complex's fourteen other gates by the immense projecting tower by which it was accompanied. Compared to this tower, the doorway through which one passed to enter the temple was actually rather unimposing. A long antechamber led up to a pair of open stone "doors," through these was an even longer passageway which was lined by twenty fluted columns carved to imitate the reed bundles that had been used in more traditional Egyptian architecture. Each column, made up of a series of drums, was attached to the side of the passageway by a short wall, a fact which seems to imply the builders' lack of confidence in their new medium. The alcoves these walls created likely contained statues of the pharaoh—perhaps one for every nome (administrative province) in Upper and Lower Egypt. Four of these alcoves led to other passageways; however, archaeologists rectify this by suggesting that there may have been less nomes at the beginning of the Old Kingdom Period. In keeping with the skeuomorphic theme, the passageway featured a ceiling that had been carved to look as though it were made of wooden logs. At the very end of the skeuomorphic passageway was a small vestibule that was framed by the four pairs of fluted columns that supported its ceiling. This vestibule's sole purpose seems to have been to give the funerary procession a bit of space to reorganize itself before it proceeded through the permanently open stone door and into the complex's great courtyard.

The complex's sprawling great courtyard was likely another replica of a location within the royal palace—this time, the area replicated seems to have been the area of the palace where Djoser made public displays to both his own people as well as dignitaries from foreign lands. Towards the southern side of the pyramid was a throne dais that could be accessed by either a set of stairs or a ramp. In front of this dais, near the center of the courtyard, were two pairs of structures shaped like horseshoes—the same architectural arrangement that is depicted on a number of artefacts from the Early Dynastic Period. It is believed that these structures somehow symbolized a scene from the Heb-Sed ceremony.

It is evident from his pyramid complex that Djoser was especially concerned with the significance of ritual. In Egypt (and elsewhere) it was believed that the order of the world was directly correlated to the king's physical prowess—namely, his valor, his virtue, and his virulence. One way for a pharaoh to prove that he was apt to rule was for him to ritually beat back the boundaries of Egypt or make a sacrifice to all the gods in the Egyptian pantheon. By the early dynastic period, all of these rituals had come to be performed in a single open space, adjacent to the royal palace, which could be filled with whatever structures were necessary for the performance of a given ritual. In mirroring this space in his mortuary complex, Djoser undoubtedly wished to prove the permanence of these rites—in this courtyard his ka would perform them for all eternity. The underlying message seems unmistakable: with Djoser as pharaoh, the era of chaos and instability had ended. As long as Djoser's pyramid complex stood, Egypt was to be governed by order, and that order was to be imposed by none other than the pharaoh.

In the southwest corner of the complex's Great Courtyard was a dummy building that has come to be known as the Token Palace. This structure was most likely meant to be a representation of the temporary pavilion that would have been set up so that the pharaoh could refresh himself at certain points during long, tiring, and undoubtedly hot ritual performances. The exterior of the Token Palace façade was decorated so that it imitated reed matting and featured a frieze of cobras poised as though about to strike. This was the image of the uraeus—a symbol of Wadjet, the goddess who was believed to patronize and protect the pharaoh. The same symbol was found on the royal headgear; here, the cobra sits on the forehead of the pharaoh, always ready to lash out at anyone who dared oppose him. Though the building itself was almost entirely solid masonry, it did have one entrance leading to a small room on its northern side. Some believe that this room contained a statue of the pharaoh (as would a sedab); others believe that it held the crowns of Upper and Lower Egypt.

The Great Courtyard was just one of many important ceremonial areas within the Djoser pyramid complex. During the Heb-Sed festival, the (living) pharaoh was traditionally double-coroneted at that chapels which belonged to the gods of both Lower and Upper Egypt. At some point in the early history of Ancient Egypt, the pharaoh probably went to visit the gods at their traditional homes; however, by Djoser's time, the gods had evidentially taken to meeting the pharaoh in the open ritual area that had been set aside next to the royal palace for just such purposes. Thus for the Heb-Sed festival, temporary reed structures were erected to serve as chapels. Djoser elected to represent these makeshift chapels in his pyramid complex. Djoser's chapels, of course, were carved from unyielding stone rather than transient reed.

This Heb-Sed court was accessed by a long passageway located to the north of the main entrance passage. This passageway grants entrance to the Heb-Sed court at the court's south-eastern corner. The entrance to another building of unknown purpose was located immediately to the left of the entrance to the Heb-Sed court. The courtyard itself was a long rectangle which was designed so as to direct one's focus to the low platform that sat at its southern end. From this platform, the pharaoh's ka—likely represented by a pair of statues—could make its ascent to a double throne with two kiosks via one of two sets of steps. Dummy "chapels" (blocks of near-solid masonry) lined the longer sides of the courtyard—those on the west side were cut in the tradition of Upper Egypt, while those on the east side were characteristic of the Lower Egyptian Delta. At the forefront of each of these dummy chapels stood a small courtyard, divided by a screen wall into two compartments. A permanently open stone door, replete with carved pivots and hinges, stood to provide entry. The side walls of the inner courtyards featured carved renditions of the wooden fences that were traditionally included in the erection of contemporary Hed-Sed shrines.

The amount of careful construction that clearly marked the construction of these chapels is all the most astonishing given their intentional lack of functionality. The western side of the Heb-Sed court featured no less than thirteen chapels of two essential styles. The first was characterized by a flat roof with torus molding at its corners and a curved overhang (at its peak. As with all structures built within the Djoser pyramid complex, this chapel was a stone replication of some unknown traditional model—in this case, the model must have been a chapel made from reeds and supported by woven reed bundles. In the middle of this chapel model's façade, a false door sits within a recess beneath an overhanging fringe. Just around the corner on the north side, a deeper niche provided a repository for offerings. This type of chapel was connected with Anubis, the jackal god of the dead.

The other chapels on the Heb Sed court's western side were constructed in the style of the "great house" chapels that had come to characterize Predynastic Upper Egypt. Traditionally, these chapels were built with a light, wood-framed structure that featured a low vaulted roof supported by three engaged fluted columns. Some suggest that these remarkable columns were originally meant to be representations of the stems of a type of hogwood known as the Heracleum giganteum, while others maintain that they were replications of wooden posts which had been shaped by an adze. Both would agree that the distinctive capitals of these columns were exquisite. Each capital was formed so that a set of pendent leaves—or the dead heads of a hogwood flower—framed an abacus, which was the top block and the primary support of the ridgepoles, which must have projected well away from the chapel's façade. The sockets likely held images of whatever god or goddess was to be worshipped at that temple. At the middle of these chapels' facades stood a doorway which offered access to a small room, the ceiling of which was made up of stone rafters carved so as to imitate palm logs. At the back of these tiny rooms could be found a small niche with a double-curved shrine roof. In at least two of these chapels, a steep stairway led up to a large niche that almost certainly must have held a statue to collect the offerings he was given. Three caryatid statues of a mummiform Djoser found lying on the ground in this courtyard attest to this theory.

Opposing these on the eastern side of the courtyard were twelve shrines constructed in the Delta tradition. These featured vaulted roofs, though these were not supported by any columns at all. Instead, their hallmark is a distinctive, fan-shaped cornice. Like their counterparts to the west, they featured a small courtyard, though this courtyard did not have any niches for statues. All of the chapels on the eastern side of the Heb Sed court had an entranceway on their southern façade; this entrance led to a small, niched chamber. The last of these chapels housed the truncated feet that had once belonged to a set of statues made in the image of a family—two children and two adults. It is believed that this set of statues represented Djoser and his principal queen as the rulers of Lower and Upper Egypt.

At the southwest corner of Djoser's Heb-Sed court was an open passageway. Following this around the corner led to a building that lay at the rear of the yard's western chapels. Accordingly, the rear corner of the last western chapel was rounded, seemingly so that there was plenty of room to maneuver a bulky object such as a carrying chair. The external appearance of this building suggests that it bore some relation to a sah netjer shrine; accordingly, it has been suggested that this building was intended to be a temple for the god Osiris. In marked contrast to most of the dummy structures in the Djoser complex, this shrine had actual rooms. The building could be entered from both the middle of its south wall and again immediately around the corner on the east side. As with most other doors in the complex, the doors were made entirely of stone and stood, permanently open, on the inside of the building's walls.

The first room of this unknown building was a small, two-columned hypostyle hall. Both the columns of this hypostyle hall and the single column of the antechamber next door were made to look like papyrus bundles and stood attached to the side wall. On the western side of the building consisted of a set of variously sized rooms—the purpose of these rooms is entirely unknown. The main focal point of the building's western side was a square room that featured a niche in its northern wall. Pilasters flanked the niche on both sides. Above it was a frieze inscribed with djed (endurance) symbols. This is the type of niche that would have once contained a statue of Djoser. The layout of this building is so characteristic of later temples that it is perhaps too easy to simple think of it as a temple; however, many Egyptologists believe that the suite of rooms were intended to be a replication of the rooms in which Djoser would have rested and changed clothes in over the course of the Heb-Sed festival. The rooms of this enigmatic building were sized similarly to those that must have accommodated the dining areas, sleeping compartments, and toilet facilities used by Djoser during his Heb-Sed.

At the northwestern corner of the Heb-Sed court was a narrow passageway which granted access to two long courtyards. A north-south wall featuring still another permanently opened stone door separated these two courtyards. At the very end of the eastern courtyard was a structure that is referred to as the House of the South; the western courtyard features a corresponding House of the North. Archaeologists believe that these structures were intended to be stone representations of still more pavilions that Djoser would have visited during his Heb-Sed festival—this time, the Red House of the Delta and the White House of Upper Egypt. Structurally, the architecture of these two houses was reminiscent of the architecture of the chapels on the western side of the Heb-Sed court. The House of the South was constructed with a similar vaulted roof and fluted, tapered columns that featured magnificent pendant, leaf-like capitals. The building's corners were supported by ribbed pilasters placed beside two fluted semi-circular shafts. The doorway to the House of the South was placed noticeably off center, clinging to one of the fluted columns. Above this doorway was a kheker frieze that appears to have been modeled upon the fringe of a carpet or mat.

Most of the House of the South was nothing more than a solid chunk of masonry; however, the doorway did lead into a long, narrow passageway that eventually arrived at a small cruciform chamber that featured niches carved into the shape of hut-shrines which at one point may have held the crowns of Upper Egypt. The courtyard of the House of the South was enclosed by a wall that was decorated with alternating buttresses and niches on its eastern and southern sides. On the eastern wall, one particularly large niche framed a singular column with a lotus capital—this must have been intended to symbolize Upper Egypt. In the southwestern corner of the courtyard was another set of horseshoe shaped markers, much the same as the ones in the Great Court. The layout of the House of the North was quite similar; however, its courtyard was significantly smaller. Instead of columns with the leaf-like capitals reminiscent of Upper Egypt, the columns of the House of the North were papyriform in homage to the plant form by which the Delta region was so often characterized.

The northern section of the Djoser pyramid complex was devoted to a large, open space known simply as the northern courtyard. The function of this courtyard remains unknown; archaeologists can't even be sure whether it was a dump site or a solar temple. A large, rectangular block of stone—15 meters across—carved out of bedrock and faced with limestone sat at the far end of the courtyard so that it faced the main pyramid burial chamber. On top of this stone was an 8 meter setting that may have been intended to be the setting for a benben stone—a stone meant to represented the sacred stone at Heliopolis upon which the sun's rays were believed to have first fallen. All that is readily apparent about the northern court of the Djoser pyramid complex is that it was never completed—it was the last part of the pyramid complex to have been built, and its construction was more than likely cut short by the pharaoh's death.

In all, when it was finished, the pyramid was a stairway to heaven upon which the pharaoh Djoser could ascend into the next life. It was a design that would often be repeated and improved upon, and it gave birth to an ancient industry dedicated to the afterlife, one that would leave an indelible mark on Egyptian life as well as death.

Djoser was the first Egyptian pharaoh to have taken on any kind of a monumental building project whatsoever, let alone a project of such unprecedented scope and nature, so the logistical problems that would have arisen in such a construction project would have been equally unprecedented. Suddenly, materials, supplies, and men had to be transported to Saqqara from all over Egypt, and once there, the thousands of men that would have been needed to work on such a large project required not only food and housing but training as well, since most had no experience whatsoever working with the material Djoser wanted them to use. Thus almost overnight Egypt saw the creation of a class of men whose sole purpose was to be able to handle such large and complicated problems. These men would have been able to apply the same kind of managerial knowledge to other projects of similar scale, such as organizing a large trading expedition or planning the invasion of a foreign nation.

The political benefits of such a monumental building project cannot be overstated. Upon its completion, Djoser's pyramid complex was, of course, an effective piece of propaganda, attesting to the stone-like permanence of the central government over a united Upper and Lower Egypt. At the same time, it was actually the process of building the complex that really solidified this message, because few things are more threatening than idle hands to an already tenuous political situation, and Djoser would have surely recognized the potential danger of having hundreds of thousands of farmers with plenty of extra time on their hands while the Nile was in its annual period of flooding. Commissioning the labor of these men for a pyramid project guaranteed that these men would be too busy to have time getting caught up in things like political unrest. Furthermore, it put men from all over Egypt on the governmental payroll, ensuring that the entire nation was equally dependent on the central government. So long as the pyramid industry was successful, the central government knew that it would not have to worry anymore about the threat of civil unrest.

Thus, the practice of building monumental pyramid complexes became standard among Djoser's successors in the third and subsequent dynasties. Of the four pharaohs believed to have ruled after Djoser in the third dynasty, two attempted to build step-pyramids in the same style. Neither of these third dynasty structures was ever completed; nevertheless, even the ruins of these abandoned pyramid projects attest to the near-overnight emergence of a pyramid industry at Memphis at the end of the Early Dynastic Period. Indeed, this pyramid industry would continue to define Memphis throughout the entirety of the golden age that the city would enjoy during the fourth and fifth dynasties.

The next great innovation in pyramid building happened under the reign of Sneferu (~2613 - ~2589 B.C.E.). Sneferu had been tasked with finishing the pyramid of Meidum, a seven-stepped pyramid that had been begun by Sneferu's father Huni. Under Sneferu, this seven-stepped pyramid was enlarged to an eight-stepped pyramid, and the steps were filled in and covered with a smooth outer facing in order to turn it into what is known as a "true" pyramid. Unfortunately, the stresses were not calculated correctly, and the structure collapsed. Many Egyptologists believe that the collapse of the Meidum pyramid served as the catalyst for the change in angle that would come to be seen as the next major step in the evolution of pyramid construction, similar to Djoser's initial construction of his step pyramid at Saqqara.

The Meidum pyramid

Sneferu's "bent pyramid" was one of the most unusual pyramids in Ancient Egypt. It was the first pyramid to have been directly connected to a valley temple. Constructed of fine white limestone, the valley temple of the Bent Pyramid had its entrance in the middle of its southern façade. Inside were three equally sized sections. The southern section featured four storerooms, their walls decorated with representations of personified mortuary estates—Upper Egyptian estates on the eastern wall, Lower Egyptian estates on the western. The northern part of the Bent Pyramid's valley temple featured a portico containing ten undecorated limestone pillars; these were painted red and arranged in two rows. The walls of this northern section were inscribed with bas-reliefs in which Sneferu could be seen participating in all the rituals of the Heb-Sed festival. Six deep niches were carved into the rear of the portico—each apparently once having had its own wooden door—to hold six statues of a walking Sneferu. The northern walls, constructed from gigantean limestone monoliths, were similarly decorated with the image of the pharaoh wearing the crowns of both Upper and Lower Egypt. This valley temple was surrounded by a mudbrick enclosure wall, and it was within this wall that the priests of Sneferu's mortuary cult would continue to make their homes until well into the Middle Kingdom period.

The Bent pyramid

People reached the Bent Pyramid complex by following a causeway out of the southwestern corner of the valley temple. This causeway, paved with limestone blocks, proceeded along an irregular path until it connected with a courtyard enclosed by the huge yellowish-gray limestone wall of the main pyramid complex. At the foot of the eastern wall stood a cult chapel constructed entirely of fine white limestone. Within this chapel was an altar in the form of the hetep (peace) symbol. The southern wall featured bas-relief inscriptions of Sneferu's name and many titles.

Originally, the Bent Pyramid was built upon a soft layer of slaty clay, but this and the relative lack of care with which its masonry was originally laid meant that the stability of the pyramid's structure was severely compromised. Fortunately, the builders recognized these errors quickly enough that they were able to implement a few corrective changes. In fact, the Bent Pyramid actually went through three major alterations from its original design plan. The original designed called for a structure that was angled at approximately 60 degrees. Before long, this was changed to a slightly gentler slope of 55 degrees—this required an enlargement of the pyramid's base. During these early phases of construction, builders attempted to lay the courses of the pyramid's core so that the stones sloped inward, as was the traditional method. This slight change in slope, however, did not prove to be enough to ensure the stability of the structure.

By the time the Bent Pyramid had reached a height of about 45 meters, the angle of its slope was reduced more dramatically—this time to an angle of about 45 degrees. This effectively reduced the mass of the pyramid's upper portions, which in turn reduced the load the superstructure had to bear. It was at this point in the construction of the Bent Pyramid that the builders began to lay the stone courses horizontally (instead of inwardly), as they had realized that these inward sloping layers of the pyramid's core actually increased the amount of stress within the structure.

The Bent Pyramid could be entered through either of two entrances. On the north side, an entrance lay about twelve meters above the ground. This entrance led to a descending corridor; this corridor led to a subterranean antechamber that featured a high corbel vault ceiling of limestone slabs. From this antechamber, a steep stairway provided ascent into a burial chamber with a similar ceiling. A short passageway led out of the southwestern corner of this burial chamber to a vertical shaft which was exactly aligned with the pyramid's vertical axis.

Much higher up on the western face of the Bent Pyramid the structure's second entrance. Like the first entrance, this led into a descending corridor; however, this descending corridor contained two portcullis barriers. Eventually, the descending corridor off the second entranceway ended in an "upper chamber," which featured still another corbel vault ceiling made of limestone slabs. In the side walls of this chamber were openings that contained cedar beams, and the lower portion of the chamber had been filled with rough limestone masonry. The exact function of these beams and masonry is still unknown. Given that this chamber contained a crude red pigment inscription bearing the cartouche of Sneferu, some Egyptologists believe that Sneferu was buried in this chamber; however, most believe that this chamber was never actually used for this purpose.

The chambers that could be accessed by the western entrance were higher than the chambers that could be accessed by the northern entrance; however, a single narrow, irregular tunnel that was carved roughly into the core of the pyramid connected both sets of substructures. This tunnel appears to have been constructed after both sets of substructures had already been completed. As the rooms of all the subterranean chambers were oriented north-south, most Egyptologists agree that that the substructures and their connecting tunnel represented the builders' efforts to reconcile traditional Egyptian theology with the newly emerging trend of sun worship that had inspired the east-west orientation of the Bent Pyramid as a while. Some Egyptologists maintain, however, that these rooms were constructed to serve a purpose similar to that of the South (Secondary) Tomb of Djoser.

A small mudbrick chapel was attached to the northern face of the Bent Pyramid. Along the southern axis was a smaller cult pyramid which contained its own substructure that could be accessed through a ground-level entrance on its northern side. As in the main pyramid, the entrance to the substructure of this secondary pyramid led first to a descending corridor and from this ascends to another small chamber with still another corbel vaulted ceiling. On the eastern side of this cult pyramid, another small chapel held an alabaster altar flanked by two five meter limestone monoliths inscribed with Sneferu's name and titles.

Sneferu was not content with the Bent Pyramid. It seems he was ardent in his desire to build a true pyramid, so he was greatly displeased when he had to change the angle of the Bent Pyramid in order to prevent the entire structure from collapsing. Sneferu therefore abandoned the Bent

Pyramid and commissioned the construction of still another pyramid, the angle of which matched the uppermost section of the Bent Pyramid: about 43 degrees. This second attempt at a true pyramid resulted in a structure that is now known as the Red Pyramid due to the red limestone of which its core was constructed. Originally, however, it was coated with a fine, white limestone and known by the name "Sneferu Shines." The Red Pyramid is the third largest pyramid in Egypt. Its blocks were often dated; from these, it is possible to deduce that the entire structure took approximately seventeen years to complete.

The Red pyramid

The entrance to the Red Pyramid was cut into the pyramid's northern face. As in the Bent Pyramid, this entrance opened into a descending corridor that led to a chamber with a corbel vaulted ceiling. A corridor off the southwestern corner of this chamber led up to a second chamber with another vaulted corbel roof—this sat directly below the apex of the Red Pyramid. An opening cut into the southern wall of this second chamber led to a third chamber with still another vaulted corbel roof. There was a mortuary temple on the eastern side of the Red Pyramid which seems to have been built hastily upon the death of Sneferu. This mortuary temple appears to have contained a satellite series of storerooms, a pink granite false door, and reliefs depicting Sneferu as he participated in the Heb-Sed festival.

Sneferu was obviously a prolific builder, and Egyptologists believe that he ordered more stone and brick to be erected than did any other pharaoh. There can be no doubt that he passed his love of building on to his descendants. Sneferu's son and successor, Khufu, (2589 B.C.E to 2566 B.C.E.) was responsible for the construction of the immortal Great Pyramid of Giza. Khufu's son, Khafre, and grandson, Menkaure, went on to adorn the Great Pyramid with three building projects of their own: the Pyramid of Khafre, the Pyramid of Menkaure, and Menkaure's iconic Great Sphinx.

To this day, the Great Pyramid of Giza is still something of an architectural marvel. Though it did not have the honor of being the first true pyramid to have been constructed in Egypt, it was nevertheless the most spectacular with respect to its size (it would remain the tallest structure on earth until the 19th century), the accuracy of its measurements, and the technical development seen in its construction. Even the ancient Greeks remarked that the Great Pyramids had the appearance of a sudden creation, "as though they had been made by some god and set down bodily in the surrounding sands."

The Great Pyramid of Giza

Over two million blocks of stone were used in the construction of the Great Pyramid, and each block weighed no less than two tons. These blocks were carved to such a degree of perfection that workers were able to construct the entire pyramid without using an ounce of cement or mortar. Though it was not perceivable until aerial photographs could be taken of the structure, the seemingly flat sides of the Great Pyramid are actually concave, a design detail which would have added to the monument's integrity and ensured that none of its blocks would ever slip out of place.

Though the scale of the Great Pyramid was entirely unprecedented, the structure was nevertheless comprised of the same discretionary elements that made up any traditional pyramid. Thus the entrance to the Great Pyramid, located on its northern face and seemingly inspired by the entrance to the Bent and Red Pyramids, provided access to a descending entrance corridor that led down into an ascending corridor, which, in turn, led up to the Pyramid's Grand Gallery. Three blocks of pink granite—weighing a staggering seven tons each—sealed the passage to the Grand Gallery in ancient times. Supporting the immense weight of this masonry were four hollow stones which are known architecturally as girdle stones.

The Grand Gallery of the Great Pyramid was an architectural masterpiece in its own right. It featured a seven-layered corbel vaulted ceiling. Each block of this corbelled ceiling was carefully placed so that it projected out several centimeters—this created a stunning visual effect, but, more importantly, it ensured that the weight of the monument was adequately dissipated. Flanking the sides of the Grand Gallery were a set of low ramps. Carved into these ramps were twenty-seven squares which corresponded precisely with the twenty-seven niches that had been carved into the Gallery's side walls. It is believed that these may have once held wooden beams that could have once aided the transportation of the building materials that were used in the pyramid's construction.

Along the western wall of the Great Gallery was a small hole located just above the door—this was known as the escape shaft, and it led to a corridor that extended well under the pyramid. Rough foot holes carved into the sides of this shaft have led some Egyptologists to believe that it was once used to provide a means of escape for the men who were tasked with lowering the giant granite blocks into the ascending entrance chamber after the burial rites had at last been completed; however, some believe that the shaft simply existed so that the workers who dug the underground chamber would have access to fresh air. Many simply maintain that this chamber represented nothing more than a preliminary stage of construction.

At the end of the descending corridor was another passageway that led to an incomplete niche and a rock cut chamber, also clearly unfinished, as no protective blocks were ever placed at its entrance. Egyptologists have noted that this entrance of this chamber was too small to allow for the passage of a sarcophagus; therefore, there is no way it could have ever been intended to be used as a burial chamber, even though the descending corridor would imply such a function.

A horizontal passage at the lower end of the Great Gallery offered entrance to the misnamed "Queen's Chamber." This chamber, located at on the pyramid's twenty-fifth course of masonry, was made of exquisitely finished limestone blocks and featured a gabled ceiling. The walls of the Queen's Chamber were not only uninscribed but utterly bare. A corbel-ceilinged niche sits at the corner of its eastern walls—this may well have held a statue of Khufu or his ka, It is highly possible that this chamber was at once point sealed off; if so, it would have been transformed into a serdab, the room which was reserved for the pharaoh's ka (as seen in Djoser's Step Pyramid Complex). Though the precise function of the Queen's Chamber has never been determined, archaeologists are certain that no queens were ever buried in the Queen's Chamber.

Within the Queen's Chamber were two "air shafts" which the builders had bricked up so well that they remained undiscovered until well into the nineteenth century. A robot sent to explore the southern shaft in 1993 found that it ended with a small slab of Tura limestone that had been inserted with two large pieces of copper. An identical door was later found in the northern shaft. No one has been able to figure out the purpose of these shafts and doors. Equally baffling to Egyptologists were three other bizarre objects found inside the Queens Chamber—a wooden slat, a granite sphere, and a copper object made in the form of a swallow's tail.

Closer to the top of the Great Pyramid was a room known as the King's Chamber. Its door was formed by another (slightly smaller) set of three pink granite monoliths. Indeed, the entire room was made of pink granite slabs. The room itself was a stunning architectural feat, as it had to be built in such a way that it would be able to resist the astonishing amount of pressure bearing down on it from the masonry above. Composed of only nine solid blocks, the flat granite roof of the Kings Chamber was able to support a staggering four hundred tons of masonry. In order to accomplish such a feat, the builders had to first construct five relief chambers. These were no more than a couple feet high; their sides were constructed of granite and limestone, and their ceilings were constructed of rough pink granite. In order to best support the immense weight of the masonry, the higher chambers were designed with saddle shaped ceilings. As these relief chambers were never intended to be seen, their walls bear some fascinating marks, including a cattle census taken seventeen years into the reign of Khufu.

The King's Chamber contains a massive, red granite sarcophagus that weighs in at an impressive 3.75 tons. Given its heavy weight, this sarcophagus was likely placed in the King's Chamber during the chamber's construction. Like so many other sarcophagi of the Early Dynastic and Old Kingdom periods, Khufu's sarcophagus was a simple flat-sided box that featured a groove on the inside of its lid. This groove supported the lid. One side was left open in order to allow for the placement of the lid; once the lid had been set in place, three pins ensured that it was sealed in place. In a stark contrast to the masonry by which it was surrounded, Khufu's sarcophagus was not well-finished. Its exterior bears obvious saw marks, and there appear to be numerous places on its northwestern corner in which the saw cut too deeply. The sarcophagus is also marred with several drill holes; though the masons apparently tried to smooth these over, they were never able to fully remove them. As the sarcophagus cover and the mummy contained therein have never been found, many claim that the King's Chamber was never intended to be a burial chamber. In fact, if it was a burial chamber, it would have been the first time a burial chamber was positioned above (rather than below) a pyramid's entrance.

Thus, even as the Great Pyramid has stood for the better part of four millennia, it is still unknown exactly the purpose for it was constructed. Such mysteries seem only to increase the unparalleled sense of awe and reverence that Memphis and its elusive legacy inspire.

In some sense, it almost seems as though the Egyptians had at least some idea of what they had achieved with the completion of the Great Pyramids. Perhaps they may have even had some intuitive sense of how difficult it would be to construct a monument that could even stand a chance of surpassing the one they had just created. That said, for whatever reason - the historical record is (perhaps unsurprising) silent on the matter - it is clear that the by the beginning of the fifth dynasty, pyramid construction at Memphis had taken on a pace that was no longer quite as frenetic as it had been during the reign of Djoser, Sneferu, and Khufu. It's possible these pharaohs of Egypt's fifth dynasty did not wish to contend with the Great Pyramids, and these pharaohs instead elected to be buried south of Giza at Abu Sir. Of course, these pharaohs did not altogether abandon the practice of pyramid building, but their pyramids were simply noticeably smaller than those of their predecessors. The pyramids of the fifth dynasty also tended to be inferior in terms of their craftsmanship.

The pyramid industry at Memphis also changed as it began to mature and Memphis' nobles continued to find new ways to innovate. As the fifth dynasty progressed, the pharaohs of Memphis began to grow increasingly concerned with the interior elements of their pyramids. The external appearance of a pyramid was no longer as important as it once had been.

At first, the pharaohs of the fifth dynasty simply displayed a marked interest in decorating the interior surfaces of their pyramid complexes with especially fine reliefs. By the end of the fifth dynasty, however, an entirely new trend emerged when Unas (~2450 B.C.E?), the last pharaoh of the fifth dynasty, elected to inscribe the interior surfaces of his pyramid chambers at Saqqara with some 227 spells on the subject of the pharaoh's resurrection and ascension to the afterlife. It was believed that these spells would aid the newly deceased pharaoh as he ascended into the sky and help him to be received among the immortal gods; in fact, a few spells even threatened the gods who failed to comply. Long after the royal residence was removed from Memphis, and even after the pyramid was no longer the first choice for a royal tomb-form, Egypt's pharaohs would continue to incorporate these so-called Pyramid Texts into the designs of their tombs.

Pyramid Texts in Unas' funerary chamber

Memphis continued to enjoy the modest prosperity of its waning golden age into the beginning of the sixth dynasty, but by this point, however, the central government at Memphis had come to be threatened by its nomarchs, who had accumulated a considerable amount of wealth and influence. Eventually, these nomarchs had no reason to depend on the pharaoh, and some grew so powerful that they were able to raise their own armies, thereby undermining the unity that the pharaohs of the Early Dynastic Period had fostered so diligently. To make matters worse, the construction of the Great Pyramids had all but bankrupted the Egyptian government.

Memphis was able to uneasily sustain such civil unrest for almost three centuries, but a severe drought at some point between 2200 and 2150 proved too much for the struggling capital to bear. The central government was quick to collapse, and with it the capital itself. When the pharaohs of the eleventh dynasty did at last manage to reunite the fractured nation, they chose Thebes as their new capital.

Flinders Petrie's Work

Thanks to the efforts made mostly by the French in the preceding decades, the underpinnings of modern Egyptology were in place when William Matthew Flinders Petrie was born on June 3, 1853, in Kent, England to William Petrie and Anne Flinders Petrie. Although Petrie was not born into wealth (at least not by standards of the time), his family was financially stable, and there were a number of accomplished individuals on both sides of his family tree. For example, Petrie's maternal grandfather, Captain Matthew Flinders, was an explorer who became one of the first Europeans to chart the Australian coast. Besides exploring the high seas, Flinders was a bit of an inventor and scientist; he invented the Flinders Bar, which counteracts a ship's magnetism and thus helps keep the ship's compass accurate. Flinders' contributions to science and Australia were later recognized in Australia when a university was named for him (Drower 1995, 506).

Flinders

Petrie's parents met through their families and were married in 1851. William had difficulty finding work to support a family, but he eventually found work as a chemist and settled into a middle-class, English life (Drower 1995, 10). One of the things drawing Petrie's parents together was their deep belief in Christianity - although Anne was an Anglican and William was from the stricter Brethren sect, they never conflicted on doctrinal or theological issues and raised Petrie with a strong Christian faith.

Petrie's faith would follow him for his entire life and would play a large role in his early interest in ancient Egypt. Reading the Bible and anything historical in nature became young Petrie's primary interest. In some ways, he was forced to become a bookworm after contracting a serious respiratory illness at the age of 4 that later prevented him from participating in cricket, soccer, and rugby with the other boys (Drower 1995, 15). However, instead of seeing his physical limitations as a barrier, Petrie worked on developing his mind by reading and studying subjects far beyond the scope of most kids his age, and before long, his precocious talents began to pay dividends, steering him toward his eventual career.

Petrie at the age of 12

As young Petrie absorbed book after book about history, engineering, and geography, he also developed an interest in numismatics. He began collecting rare coins and quickly demonstrated a natural talent for discerning valuable coins from those less valuable and forgeries. Petrie's coin-collecting talents came to the attention of the curator of the Department of Coins and Medals at the British Museum, London, who bought several coins from him (Drower 1995, 19). With the small income he received from selling coins to the museum, Petrie was able to dedicate his time and energy to more ambitious pursuits, such as building his personal library and making his mark on the academic world.

One fascinating aspect of Petrie's life is that he was not formally educated in the same way as nearly every professional academic today. Petrie's university degrees came later in his life, and although they were certainly deservedly earned in the field, they were all technically honorary. For the most part, Petrie was auto-didactic, having learned everything he knew from books he read or personal experience. He developed his archaeological methodology through trial and error and made his greatest discoveries through his own keen sense of intuition and sharp intellect. Petrie also had a strong work ethic and was always working on a project, be it a dig in Egypt or publishing the findings from the excavation back home in England.

The project that first brought Petrie academic notoriety and respect took place in England. In the early 1870s, when Petrie was a young man in his late teens and early 20s, he began looking to make his name in the world. When most young men his age were either starting families or attending university, Petrie decided to tackle the task of measuring and surveying Stonehenge, Britain's most famous ancient monument. In 1874, Petrie took a train from his home to southwest England to survey and measure the Stonehenge monoliths, where things were quite a bit different than they are today. There was very little tourist activity to speak of, and visitors could walk right up to the monoliths and touch them, which was crucial for Petrie's project. Since there was little tourist activity, there was also no accompanying infrastructure, such as restaurants, shops, and inns, so the young scholar had to fend for himself by supplying his own food and lodging. Petrie was a lifelong ascetic when it came to comforts, choosing to live in austere and minimalistic ways. He would often camp near Stonehenge or rent cheap rooms in the area, living on meager rations.

The work seemed to be enough to sustain him, and the project proved nearly as monumental as the stones, taking Petrie until 1877 to complete. He returned in 1880 to make a midsummer observation and then set to put his findings into writing. The academic community immediately recognized Petrie's work, and his reputation as an aspiring young scholar was cemented (Drower 1995, 25).

Petrie's next destination would be his most famous. He favored his father's literal interpretation of theology and especially enjoyed reading the Old Testament books about the Exodus and the later Kingdom of Israel. The family also stayed current on theological and biblical historical literature, which is how Petrie first became acquainted with the writing of John Taylor and Charles Piazzi Smyth. Taylor was known for his book, *The Great Pyramid–Why Was It Built and Who Built It?*, which attempted to answer the riddle of the Giza Pyramids through the lens of the Bible. Taylor's central thesis was that pi had been incorporated into the Great Pyramid, proving there was a connection to God. Smyth followed Taylor's theory with his 1864 book, *Our Inheritance in the Great Pyramid,* agreeing with Taylor's thesis but adding that the Great Pyramid was much older than previously believed. Smyth added that the measurements used to construct the Great Pyramid were almost equal to the British system and that once this was accepted, a secret history of the world—past, present, and future—could be read in its measurements. He referred to the near equal British inch the Egyptians had used as the "pyramid inch" (Drower 1995, 27-29).

Piazzi Smyth

Taylor and Smyth's theories about the pyramids became quite popular in the Victorian Era and still have some adherents today, but the academic community never really paid either man serious consideration. Both men had the publication of their theories rejected by the prestigious Royal Society (Lehner 2001, 57), which put the idea of the "pyramid inch" to rest among early Egyptologists, but young Petrie determined that he needed to travel to Egypt to do a survey of the Great Pyramid himself. He expected to confirm Taylor and Smyth's theories and possibly unlock more arcane wisdom.

Petrie arrived in Egypt in November 1880, and although it was quite different than the world he was used to back in England, he took to it readily, making his way through Cairo to obtain the necessary permits to carry out a mapping survey. Things were obviously quite different for would be Egyptologists then, as the British ran the government, but the antiquities council was in the hands of French scholars. Not only was it easy for Petrie—a man with no real academic credentials—to obtain a permit to work at Giza, but he was also allowed to make one of the nearby tombs his home (Drower 1995, 38). To fund his venture, Petrie sold a number of rare coins and scarabs he had bought on the streets of Cairo to the British Museum once he had returned home (Drower 1995, 48). The museum bought the items, no questions asked.

A picture Petrie took from the tomb he called home in 1881

While 19th century scholars were trying to conceive of links between their contemporary societies and the ancient Egyptians, the truth behind the pyramids was more impressive. In fact, the Egyptians spent centuries perfecting the techniques that would lead to the construction of the Great Pyramid at Giza.

When he came to Egypt, Petrie spent his days taking measurements of the Great Pyramid, and every night, he would collate his data and write reports by the light of a lantern in the tomb. He was kept company by howling, semi-feral dogs, which he took in stride.

It did not take Petrie very long to determine that "pyramid inch" was a thing of fiction (Drower 1995, 51), but refuting Smyth's theory did nothing to dampen Petrie's newfound enthusiasm for ancient Egypt. On the contrary, he was determined to find lost temples and cities buried beneath the farmland and villages of one of the modern world's most densely populated countries. He traveled back to England by ship in the spring of 1881 and set to work on his first publication of ancient Egyptian archaeology, *The Pyramids and Temples of Gizeh*. The book was published in 1883 after his second season in Egypt, but in the meantime, he was busy making professional connections and establishing himself in England as one of the up and coming members of the second generation of Egyptologists.

In 1882, before he set out on his second season in Egypt at the age of 27, Petrie helped establish the Egypt Exploration Fund along with noted British writer Amelia Edwards (Reid 2002, 172). The Fund would support Petrie in many of his early digs, and it still exists today as the Egypt Exploration Society.

Edwards

There is no evidence to suggest that Petrie was driven by ego or that he wanted to outdo any of his colleagues. That is not to say that Petrie did not value his reputation among his peers, but that his work appears to have been driven by a genuine desire to uncover the truth. Although he was not necessarily liked by all Egyptologists of the era and few preferred to work with him, none of them criticized his motives, and few took issue with his results. Indeed, after two seasons at Giza, most Egyptologists viewed him as a legitimate scholar.

Petrie's reputation rose dramatically when he began to make numerous discoveries around 1884. Beginning in that year, Petrie discovered lost cities, pyramids, and caches of mummies that dated to the Roman occupation of Egypt. The flurry of finds was enough to place Petrie at the forefront of Egyptology by the turn of the century.

For his third season in Egypt, Petrie decided to focus his work in the Delta region, which is where he first began doing excavations. Since he was essentially the "new guy," Petrie had to take what he could get, so he began excavating at Tanis and other Delta sites (Drower 1995, 65-

82). There are numerous problems modern archeologists encounter when excavating in the Delta. The dense population, high water table, and rich, agricultural soil have combined to ensure that most of the major monuments have been buried, and even when monuments have been uncovered in the modern period, farmers who care more about feeding their families than ancient artifacts have often reused the blocks for new structures or even fertilizer (Davies and Freidman 1998, 29-30). To make matters more difficult, Petrie only had 19th century technology at his disposal, which meant using plenty of manpower and a little donkey power.

Petrie set to work excavating the Twenty-Second Dynasty capital city of Tanis with native workers recommended to him by colleagues. He learned as he went and made sure to collect, file, and categorize everything, including things most other archaeologists would have left behind, such as pottery shards.

Although Petrie's work at Tanis was important, he was looking for a more significant discovery: the city of Naucratis. Naucratis was a major Greek colony, first settled in the 7th century BCE during the Saite or Twenty-Sixth Dynasty. The Saite kings, so-named for the capital of the Delta city of Sais, invited Greek merchants and mercenaries to settle in Egypt but restricted them to a Greek quarter in Memphis and the newly built city of Naucratis in the Delta. Classical historians, most notably Herodotus, wrote about the city, but its location was lost in the ages, presumably somewhere far below a village or farm somewhere in the Delta. Petrie knew that Naucratis was somewhere in the Delta, so as he worked and traveled in the region in 1883 and 1884, he was continually looking for signs.

Finally, in late 1884, he found a stone serving as a door pivot on a modern house with the Greek name "Naucratis" inscribed on it (Drower 1995, 88). Petrie began excavations of the site and later found the Greek mercenary fort of Daphne nearby (Drower 1995, 97). Once again, getting permits for excavations was relatively easy due to the British occupation, and though he had to split his discoveries with the antiquities department, he was never hindered in his choice of sites (Reid 2002, 176).

From 1885-1887, Petrie was busy with publications. He wrote and published *Tanis: Part I* and *Tanis: Part II* in 1885 and 1887, as well as *Naucratis: Part I* (1886) and an interesting anthropological study titled *Racial Photographs from the Egyptian Monuments* (1887).

A picture of Petrie in 1886

His next target was the region in the middle of Egypt known as the Fayum, a fertile depression covering around 10,000 square miles in the Libyan Desert about 45 miles south of modern Cairo. The region became important during the Middle Kingdom (ca. 2055-1650 BCE), when the Egyptian capital was located near modern Lisht (Shaw and Nicholson 1995, 98). A number of Middle Kingdom pharaohs built their pyramids in the region, although by the modern era, most of them looked like sandhills due to their limestone casing having been removed in later periods (Lehner 2001, 174).

Petrie decided that beginning in the fall of 1887, he would uncover the remnants of some of those pyramids to learn more about the Middle Kingdom. For the next few years, he traveled up and down the Nile extensively, making observations at a number of notable sites before settling into the Fayum site known as Hawara to begin excavations. He planned to excavate one of the Middle Kingdom pyramids, which included the surrounding temple complex area, and he almost immediately made a major discovery.

Buried near the pyramid was a large cache of Roman treasures. Numerous demotic and Greek papyri were discovered, but since Petrie's language skills were minimal, he called in some of his classicist colleagues, most notably Heinrich Schliemann, the man who had discovered the lost city of Troy. It was discovered that the cache was more important than Petrie had initially thought because a copy of the *Iliad* was found among the papyrus rolls (Reid 2002, 162). Also in the cache were hundreds of mummies found in coffins with amazingly well-preserved mummy portraits, some of the most unique works of art from the Roman Period. To Petrie, they were more of a curiosity, and he enjoyed doing psychological profiles of the owners. As one writer put it, "The personalities behind the portraits intrigued him; a young lady he describes as 'tolerably good looking, and evidently thought of herself more so'; a rather plain young man 'looks as if he would have made a very conscientious hard-working curate, with a tendency to pulpit hysterics.'" (Drower 135). Petrie's witty statements and theories about the owners' personalities aside, Roman Period finds from Hawara, along with his discovery of Naucratis, represented some of the greatest Greco-Roman discoveries in Egypt. Indeed, Petrie's finds from Hawara and Naucratis would give impetus to Greco-Roman archaeology and studies in Egypt, and it would lead to the creation of the Greco-Roman Museum in Alexandria in 1895 (Reid 2002, 162).

The discovery of the Roman Period mummies caused a great stir among non-Egyptologists, but while Petrie was intrigued by the find, he was more interested in entering what was left of the pyramid that towered over his camp. Since pyramids have no inscriptions on their exteriors, Petrie would need to find a way inside to uncover the mystery, as well as the remains of anything tomb robbers missed that might have the king's name inscribed on it.

After completing his survey of the pyramid, Petrie led his team to dig through the walls of the pyramid, which paid off in January 1889 when they broke through to the main chamber. Artifacts found inside the pyramid revealed that it had once belonged to Amenemhat III (ruled 1855-1808 BCE), the sixth king of the Twelfth Dynasty (Drower 1995, 146). It was another major discovery for Petrie, as it helped to fill in many chronological blanks in ancient Egyptian history. Amenemhat III was one of the most important rulers of the Middle Kingdom and was one of the kings responsible for the increase in building activity in Fayum. It was later learned that the Hawara pyramid was actually Amenemhat III's second - and not his final - resting place (Shaw and Nicholson 1995, 28).

As Petrie viewed the burial chamber from the tunnel he dug above it, he soon learned the pyramid was built with trap doors and false tunnels, which led him to formulate it had been the inspiration for the labyrinth mentioned by classical historians such as Herodotus (Drower 1995, 146). Herodotus claimed to have visited the Egyptian labyrinth when he toured Egypt in the 5th century BCE, writing, "The pyramids, too, are astonishing structures, each one of them equal to many of the most ambitious works of Greece; but the labyrinth surpasses them. It has twelve covered courts —six in a row facing north, six south—the gates of the one range exactly fronting the gates of the other, with a continuous wall round [sic] the outside of the whole…The upper rooms, on the contrary, I did actually see, and it is hard to believe that they are the work of men; the baffling and intricate passages from room to room and from court to court were an endless wonder to me, as we passed from a courtyard into rooms, from rooms into galleries, from galleries into more rooms, and thence into yet more courtyards. The roof of every chamber, courtyard, and gallery is, like the walls, of stone. The walls are covered with carved figures, and each court is exquisitely built of white marble and surrounded by a colonnade. Near the corner where the labyrinth ends there is a pyramid, two hundred and forty feet in height, with great carved figures of animals on it and an underground passage by which it can be entered." (Herodotus, *The Histories*, II, 148)

The Greeks believed the Egyptian labyrinth to be the inspiration for the Minoan labyrinth on Crete (Lehner 2001, 183). When Petrie realized what he had discovered was not the labyrinth but just as important in pharaonic history, he devoted his energies toward excavating and publishing the pyramid. The reality is that the labyrinth Herodotus (and later Strabo) claimed to have visited was probably part of the larger pyramid complex Petrie had discovered, but it had been so completely quarried since the Roman Era that only a foundation bed of sand and some limestone chips remained (Lehner 2001, 183). Even without discovering the legendary labyrinth, Petrie had once

The late Eighteenth Dynasty is perhaps the most enigmatic period in ancient Egyptian history if not the history of the ancient Near East. Often call the "Amarna Period" for the modern village where Pharaoh Akhenaten (reigned ca. 1352-1336 BCE) made his capital, interpretations of the period by Egyptologists and lay people alike have wildly varied.

Historically speaking, Akhenaten was Nefertiti's husband and probably Tutankhamun's father, and he is most known for moving the capital to his newly-built city of Akhetaten (Amarna). Artistic conventions changed dramatically during Akhenaten's rule, as did theology, for it appears that he only worshipped the sun-disc known as the "Aten" (Shaw and Nicholson 1995, 20-21). Unfortunately, the manner in which Akhenaten's reign ended and how power was passed to his successors remains a mystery, which has led to differing theories about the king's life over the centuries. As a result, by the time Petrie became an Egyptologist, the two most popular theories concerning Akhenaten's life were that he was either a mystical vessel of esoteric wisdom (Montserrat 2003, 124-37) or the world's first monotheist (Montserrat 2003, 120-3). These two views represented popular movements of the era, as theosophy was popular among many elites and Victorian Era Christians looked for archaeological proof of the Bible. Petrie, of course, fell into the second category, so he was naturally drawn to Amarna and Akhenaten.

In the 1891-92 season, Petrie began what was perhaps his most popular dig, and to say that he was excited about working at Amarna would be an understatement. He finally got to uncover the city of the king whom he believed to be the world's first monotheist and "the most original thinker that ever lived in Egypt, and one of the greatest idealists of the world" (Drower 1995, 198). Everything about the site of Amarna/Akhetaten seemed to point to the king as the original thinker Petrie believed him to be, as the city was isolated and off the beaten track and the nearby tombs were on the east bank of the Nile instead of the standard west bank.

After a careful survey of the area, Petrie went to work with his crew and discovered the enigmatic king's palace. Although later archaeologists would work at the site for longer periods of time than Petrie, he was the first to truly "open" the site (Drower 1995, 191). As Petrie worked to uncover the secrets of Egypt's most enigmatic king, he could not escape the crowds of curious onlookers. Petrie's discovery of Akhenaten's palace attracted scores of Westerners who had heard about the find. Ever the polite English gentleman, Petrie took the time to speak with all visitors who wished to talk to him, especially the wealthy patrons who were at least partially funding the dig (Montserrat 2003, 88).

Although the existence of Amarna had been known since the early 19th century, the discovery of the so-called "Amarna Letters" brought a new wave of interest to the lost city. The Amarna Letters were made up of 380 cuneiform tablets of correspondence between the kings of Egypt, Babylon, Hatti, Assyria, and Mittani, which were the "Great Powers," and the lesser Canaanite city-states of the Levant during the Late Bronze Age. It soon became clear that the tablets formed part of a state administrative archive. The archive mostly consists of correspondence between the rulers and diplomats of the Near East nations, including those of Babylonia, Assyria, Hitti, Mitanni, Syria, Canaan, and Ancient Egypt during the reigns of Amenhotep III and Akhenaten. They have become a primary source to historians for establishing the timeline of the early New Kingdom period of Ancient Egypt, and of gaining a greater understanding of the international diplomatic and administrative framework of the period.

Many scholars of the era, including Petrie, believed the letters confirmed many aspects of the Old Testament. Petrie saw the discovery of the Amarna Letters as a good way to help his career as well as promote Amarna's public profile in particular and Egyptology in general. He wrote several essays about Amarna in popular publications, many of which were religious in nature, where he had more freedom to promote his ideas about Biblical history (Montserrat 2003, 66).

Petrie returned from Amarna as one of the premier archaeologists in the world and quickly became a promoter of Egyptology. Far from being an elitist or a snob, Petrie believed that people from all classes should be allowed to study ancient Egypt formally at major universities. A number of influential people in British society agreed with his sentiments, most notably his friend and benefactor, Amelia Edwards, whose will proposed that an endowment for the chair of Egyptology at University College, London be given to Petrie (Drower 1995, 200). Petrie would work at University College, London for most of the remainder of his life, educating several prominent third-generation British Egyptologists.

Just as he had with archaeology, Petrie threw himself into his work as an educator, developing curriculum and pedagogical ideas that are still followed by many Egyptology programs in the English-speaking world. Perhaps owing to his linguistic deficiencies and his personal and professional interests, Petrie believed the Germans should lead the way in ancient Egyptian philology while the study of material culture should be in the English purview. Petrie also encouraged the involvement of part-time scholars in the field and supported female students at University College, London (Drower 1995, 203).

Even more important than the new pedagogical philosophies introduced to Egyptology by Petrie was his system of excavation. When one looks at Petrie's system of excavation, it seems quite logical and self-evident, but in the decades prior, excavation was often chaotic and destructive. Many 19th century archeologists worked on commission, and since museums usually only paid for larger, more impressive pieces, many sites were damaged to obtain a few pieces as a result (Jeffreys 2011, 3-4). By the time Petrie got into archaeology, there were, thankfully, more restraints in place, but many still used destructive archaeological techniques.

Petrie's simple yet effective method involved first finding a location where he believed there to be a significant discovery waiting to be found, and he clearly had an uncanny talent for finding such places. Once he had decided on an excavation site and permits were in hand, he inspected the surface and sent in "basket boys" to clear the surface of debris. When pottery was found, the *quftis* (natives with archaeological experience) would take over with brushes and knives. The head *qufti* cleared away the remainder of the debris, allowing Petrie to draw or photograph everything discovered *in situ* before it was taken from the pit (Drower 1995, 216). This technique has been emulated by archaeologists from around the world in different disciplines and is still used to an extent today.

While Petrie was far from arrogant, he knew that his system of archeology was better than any other, so he published his techniques in the 1903 book *Methods and Aims in Archaeology*. The title is still read today and is required reading for anyone considering a profession in archaeology (Drower 1995, 277). Besides outlining his system, Petrie described some of the traits a good archaeologist should possess, including a strong sense of history, good organizational skills, a keen memory, and at least a minimal background in engineering (Drower 1995, 278). As Petrie continued on his career in archaeology, he further developed his techniques, combining them with emerging technologies.

With that said, there is no doubt that Petrie constantly did things his own way, which sometimes aroused scoffing and maybe a little contempt from his contemporaries. One of the things many Egyptologists found curious about Petrie was his insistence on not only excavating pottery and pottery shards but meticulously cataloging each piece, while the early second generation of Egyptologists was still very much influenced by the "bigger is better" theory adhered to by the first generation. Statues and other sizable monuments were seen as the most valuable pieces to be excavated, with smaller pieces such as *ushabtis* and other funerary artifacts coming in second. Pottery was ignored for the most part, especially when broken, but Petrie was more interested in uncovering the truths of ancient Egyptian history than he was in selling pieces to museums or making a name for himself. He knew that properly categorized pottery was the key to unlocking Egypt's often confusing chronology.

Petrie understood that pottery styles changed according to periods and could thus be used to date archaeological sites. While he was excavating the pre-dynastic site of Naqada in 1899, Petrie developed a chronological series of the pottery he discovered, even as he was unable to assign definitive dates (Drower 1995, 251-2). Petrie's system of dating sites using pottery was further developed in later decades and eventually used by archaeologists outside of the English-speaking world and the discipline of Egyptology. The system is now known as "seriation." In Cambridge, it is often referred to as the "Petrie Matrix" or "Petriefication" (Drower 1995, 252).

A picture of pottery from the Pre-Dynastic period recognizable for the black tops

Petrie was also far ahead of his time with respect to other techniques he used in the fields of archaeology and Egyptology. He was one of the first archaeologists to use X-rays to examine delicate objects such as mummies (Jeffreys 2011, 6). The X-ray examination of mummies (especially small animals) is quite common, not only in Egyptology but in other sub-disciplines of archaeology.

Petrie's efforts to educate the greater public about the importance of Amarna have already been discussed, but the need to educate people about history was a part of his overall philosophy. Since Petrie did not come from an aristocratic background, he essentially believed in the "democratization" of history and archaeology, which was a progressive concept in the 19th century. Colleagues occasionally criticized Petrie for writing about history and archaeology in popular, accessible, and exciting publications, at least when compared to the often verbose academic literature available during the period (Montserrat 2003, 11).

Although he continued to believe he would one day discover a site or document proving the historicity of the Bible, Petrie did not find that smoking gun until 1896. During the 1895-96 excavation season, Petrie was working in western Thebes, digging at what once had been the palace of King Amenhotep III (ruled ca. 1390-1352 BCE) (Drower 1999, 472). Amenhotep III was important due to the length of his reign, and also because he was Akhenaten's father.

Since many of the Amarna Letters had been addressed to and sent by Amenhotep III, Petrie hoped that more archaeological evidence would be found at his palace to verify certain details in the Old Testament. As Petrie's season wound down in the spring of 1896, he discovered a curious stela that seemed a bit out of place. Although Petrie was not a philologist, he was able to read Merenptah (reigned ca, 1213-1203 BCE), the son and successor of Ramesses II (ruled ca.

1279-1213 BCE), as the king's name in the text. This was important because many Biblical scholars and Egyptologists believe that Exodus took place during the reign of Ramesses II.

Petrie called in his friend and colleague, German philologist Wilhelm Spiegelberg, to translate the text. Petrie was pleasantly surprised to read the phrase, "Israel is wasted, bare of seed" (Lichtheim 1976, 77). Though not very detailed, for Petrie this served to confirm the historicity of the Old Testament. The text became known as the "Israel Stela" and remains the first mention of Israel in any non-Biblical text (Drower 1995, 221). Drower explained the importance: "Petrie dug and soon solved the puzzle: the temple had been built by Merneptah, the son and successor of Ramesses II, almost entirely from stone which had been plundered from the temple of Amenophis III nearby. Statues of the latter had been smashed and the pieces thrown into the foundations; fragments of couchant stone jackals, which must have once formed an imposing avenue approaching the pylon, and broken drums gave some idea of the splendour of the original temple. A statue of Merenptah himself was found—the first known portrait of this king....Better was to follow: two splendid stelae were found, both of them usurped on the reverse side by Merenptah, who had turned them face to the wall. One, beautifully carved, showed Amenophis III in battle with Nubians and Syrians; the other, of black granite, was over ten feet high, larger than any stela previously known; the original text commemorated the building achievements of Amenophis and described the beauties and magnificence of the temple in which it had stood. When it could be turned over an inscription of Merenptah recording his triumphs over the Libyans and the Peoples of the Sea was revealed; Spiegelberg came over to read it, and near the end of the text he was puzzled by one, that of a people or tribe whom Merenptah had victoriously smitten-'I.si.ri.ar?' It was Petrie whose quick imaginative mind leapt[t] to the solution: 'Israel!' Spiegelberg agreed that it must be so. 'Won't the reverends be pleased?' was his comment. At dinner that evening Petrie prophesied: 'This stele will be better known in the world than anything else I have found.' It was the first mention of the word 'Israel' in any Egyptian text and the news made headlines when it reached the English papers."

Spiegelberg

When Petrie was working and developing his system of seriation at Naqada, his primary intent was to excavate at the nearby site of Abydos, which he did from 1899-1904 and again in the 1921-22 season. Abydos was important to Petrie for a number of reasons. Today, the most visible part of the ancient site is the New Kingdom temple built by King Seti I (ruled ca. 1294-1279 BCE), but Petrie was more intrigued by less visible artifacts far below the surface. Long before the New Kingdom pharaohs built temples at Abydos, the first kings of Egypt were laid to rest at the site (Shaw and Nicholson 1995, 14). The site was first explored by Frenchman Emile Amélineau, who found nothing of value, but Gaston Maspero, director of the Egyptian antiquities council at the time, gave Petrie the concession for the 1900-1901 excavation season.

Petrie believed there were extremely important things to find beneath the sands of Abydos and conducted his excavation of what turned out to be Abydos' royal necropolis, the first one of its kind in ancient Egypt. Most subsequent royal necropolises were located near Memphis or Thebes, so the discovery of one at Abydos was big, and its importance was magnified after Petrie had collated the data from the dig. Petrie examined names associated with the tombs and compared them with other texts to build an accurate chronological list of ancient Egypt's kings from the first two dynasties, the so-called "Early Dynastic Period," which filled a large gap in the scholarship of the period (Drower 1995, 259). Before leaving Abydos during his first expedition, he also discovered the "Osireion," the cenotaph of Seti I (Drower 1995, 268). Petrie's discoveries at Abydos represented some of his last great discoveries in Egypt.

Petrie would continue to lead excavations in Egypt and later in Palestine in the early 20th century, but some of his later contributions to academia took place while he was back home in England. Petrie was always interested in how his discoveries helped clarify not only ancient Egyptian history but the history of the world in general. Petrie saw patterns in world history (perhaps owing to his mathematical and scientific mind) and came to believe that world history was a series of cycles in which nations, kingdoms, and civilizations rose and declined. He lectured and wrote about his "big picture" historical ideas in the early 20th century, eventually putting his theories in print in his 1911 book *The Revolutions of Civilization* (Drower 1995, 303). Although *Revolutions* is often overlooked by modern adherents of cyclical and "big history," it was published years before Arnold Toynbee or Oswald Spengler had published their better-known cyclical studies of world history.

Petrie's last great archaeological discovery also took place in England. In the spring of 1922, after returning from a season in Egypt, Petrie and his son John headed to southeastern England to study the mysterious Silbury Hill. Towering over the fields of quiet, southeastern England, Silbury Hill had always been a combination of enigma and pride to the people of England. Although they did not know its origins or if it was even manmade, people thought it was connected to nearby Stonehenge and Petrie firmly believed it to be a ceremonial monument built by the ancient Celts. As such, during the spring and summer, he and John set to work surveying every inch of the edifice. Through his work, Petrie determined that the structure was, indeed, manmade, although he could not speak to its function (Drower 1995, 354). Silbury Hill has been the subject of subsequent studies both academic and popular, but none have gone further beyond Petrie's discovery that it was made by people.

Since Petrie was what one would call a "workaholic," nearly all parts of his social and family life were connected to his career. His vacations were usually "workcations," whether surveying Silbury Hill with his son or visiting sites in Rome on his way to or from Egypt, but Petrie went out of his way to involve his family in all of his work and adventures, even if his children were not as receptive to the overtures as his wife. For much of his young adulthood, Petrie never thought much about starting a family, as he did not believe he had the time or money to do so, but by the time he had entered his 40s, Petrie was a respected scholar who was finally making enough money.

When Petrie met Hilda Mary Isobel Urlin, things were a bit awkward. He had never been serious with a woman, and there was a bit of an age difference between them, as he was 43 and she was 26. Still, the two got along well, and she proved to be an intellectual match. Not only could Hilda follow what Petrie was talking about in terms of his work, but she showed genuine interest. The couple married in November 1896 and left immediately for Egypt's excavation season (Drower 1995, 238-9). Hilda proved to be quite the trooper when she accompanied Petrie on digs. Although Petrie lived in shacks instead of tents while in Egypt, the accommodations were still quite primitive compared to what Hilda was used to back home.

Far from the stereotype of the prissy, English schoolgirl, Hilda not only took well to the austere life on a Petrie dig, but she seemed to relish it as much as her husband. Not only did the couple share a love of learning and ancient Egypt, but also the same faith, which is probably how Hilda was able to handle the living conditions better than most. She was given increasing responsibility each year while accompanying Petrie on digs, learned Arabic, and was particularly skilled at drawing, all of which allowed her to contribute to Petrie's publications (Drower 1995, 243). Hilda also helped Petrie edit his publications and displayed a particular aptitude for public speaking. When the couple was in England, Hilda would often give lectures to archaeology organizations or on the UCL campus about her husband's recent discoveries. The public enjoyed her comfortable speaking style and witty nature (Drower 1995, 254).

Petrie and his wife in 1903

Petrie enjoyed marriage and truly loved Hilda, but he wanted to pass his legacy on to his children, preferably a son. In 1907, Hilda gave birth to a boy the couple named John (Drower 1995, 307). Like his father and grandfather, young John was inquisitive and showed academic promise from an early age. He was quite good at math and enjoyed accompanying his father to museums and surveying Silbury Hill, but he did not share his father's enthusiasm for archaeology or Egypt. Petrie was a bit upset and did what he could to push his son to follow in his footsteps, but to no avail. John later enlisted in the army and served in World War II. He was captured at Dunkirk and spent most of the war in a German prisoner-of-war-camp (Drower 1995, 420). After the war, John returned to England to teach math for the remainder of his life and developed what is known as the "Petrie Polygon" (Drower 1995, 427). John Petrie died in 1972.

The couple also had a daughter, Ann, who was born in 1909 (Drower 1995, 311). Like her older brother, Ann was a precocious student who showed little interest in archaeology or Egyptology. When Petrie was on excavations, both children stayed behind with either their mother or family members, but during World War I, when Petrie stayed in England, the children bonded with their father (Drower 1995, 335). When Ann went to college, Petrie hoped she'd embark on a study of the ancient world, but her interests brought her to the Italian language and modern Italian history. Ann would later use her background to work for British intelligence during World War II (Drower 1995, 420). She died in 1989.

By all accounts, Petrie was a good husband and father, if not a different model of what one might expect today. Despite his conservative political beliefs, he was fairly open and liberal when it came to his wife, which included encouraging her to pursue her interests and promoting them alongside his own. It helped that his wife's professional and personal interests aligned with his, but he was clearly progressive for the time in terms of gender relations.

His relationship with his children was a bit more traditional. Petrie expected his children to follow in his footsteps, and when they did not, it led to tension. Part of the problem may have been due to the fact that Petrie was in his 50s when he first became a father, which no doubt led to a generation gap. Petrie's children mostly grew up in the 1920s, which became known as the "Roaring Twenties" for a good reason. The Petrie children grew up with telephones, radios, and automobiles in a culture more secular and permissive than anything Petrie could have imagined in the 19th century.

If there were one theme to characterize Petrie's professional and personal life, it would be order. The way he excavated in Egypt and Palestine brought him great success and fame, and this style of order was also apparent in his daily life. Whether in the Middle East or England, Petrie awoke every day at the same time, ate the same food, and retired for the evening around the same time. When he was traveling to and from Egypt, his itinerary was well-planned, and any deviation caused him consternation. Petrie also tried to follow an orderly path in his relationship with his children, although that did not quite go as he had planned.

His love of order also extended to his political beliefs. Petrie was a lifelong supporter of conservative causes and political parties, and though he was never very forward with his political beliefs around friends and colleagues, he would discuss them when asked. Many of Petrie's political and social beliefs would not be considered politically correct today and might even be considered offensive, but they were mainstream in the early 20th century. With respect to Petrie's theory of cyclical civilization, he believed that nations, kingdoms, and civilizations were overcome by foreign ethnic groups only after the nation had grown weak, something he believed to be the result of breeding. In other words, Petrie was an advocate of eugenics, which he outlined in his 1907 book, *Janus in Modern Life* (Drower 1995, 303). To Petrie, biology was a cultural determinant that affected the form of a nation or civilization, how powerful the nation or civilization would be, and how long the nation or civilization would last (Reid 2002, 178). Petrie, therefore, argued that not only should the best elements of society be promoted to breed and have more children, but that the criminal and other problematic elements of society should be discouraged from having children (Drower 1995, 303).

Petrie was a senior citizen in the 1920s, but he was still very active. He still worked in the Middle East but was delegating more work to others. He continued to write and lecture in England, promoting UCL's Egyptology program and Egyptology and archaeology in general.

Petrie became a legend in his own time, gaining wider and more prestigious recognition. He was knighted in 1922, an honor he certainly cherished but one that he liked to avoid discussing (Drower 1995, 358).

Petrie at Abydos in 1922

One of the more interesting facets of Petrie's life beyond what he contributed to archaeology and Egyptology was the amazing number of people he met, worked with, and befriended over the course of his lifetime. They included many luminaries in the fields of archaeology and Egyptology, but there were also statesmen, philosophers, and other famous people in Petrie's social circle.

One of the famous scholars Petrie worked with was Archibald (A.H.) Sayce (1845-1933), a well-published philologist who was a pioneer in Hittite studies in the 19th century. Petrie met Sayce at Oxford in the summer of 1881 and immediately formed a strong professional and personal bond with the Assyriologist. The two men complemented each other perfectly in their professional lives, as Petrie helped Sayce understand the nuances of ancient architecture and building techniques, while Sayce helped Petrie translate ancient texts (Drower 1995, 51).

Over the course of his long career of excavating and teaching, Petrie mentored a number of students who'd go on to establish impressive reputations in the field. Francis Griffith was one of Petrie's student archaeologists when Naucratis was discovered (Drower 1995, 85), and Griffith would later go on to be an influential Egyptologist and start the Griffith Institute, which still publishes Egyptology-related titles.

Petrie's most famous student was Howard Carter, the archaeologist who is famous for discovering King Tutankhamun's tomb in the Valley of the Kings in 1922. Carter got his start in archaeology by studying the Amarna Period when he worked for Petrie as a student there in 1892 (Drower 1995, 187). The young Carter worked on Petrie's team as an artist, copying the artifacts they found, but while Petrie seemed to like him, he had his doubts about Carter's archaeological abilities. Petrie wrote of him, "Mr. Carter is a good-natured lad whose interest is entirely in painting and natural history: he only takes on this digging as being on the spot and convenient to Mr. Amherst, and it is of no use to me to work him up as an excavator." (Drower 1995, 194).

Alan Gardiner was another giant in the field of Egyptology who worked with and befriended Petrie. Born in 1879, Gardiner was Petrie's junior in age, but the men were equals in academic and intellectual pursuits. Although both men were influential Egyptologists, Gardiner focused his studies on philology while Petrie was primarily interested in archaeology and history. Gardiner would write a grammar textbook that became the premier text for English-speaking students and is still used today in many universities. While the two men's expertise in Egyptology were different, they complimented each other. Petrie would often contact Gardiner for help translating the texts he discovered, and Gardiner would ask for Petrie's advice regarding material culture (Drower 1995, 326).

Petrie's contact with Amelia Edwards was extensive through the Egypt Exploration Fund and somewhat ephemeral with Schliemann, who was coming to the end of his career and life when Petrie worked with him at Hawara (Drower 1995, 138). With Breasted, it was more a case of what could have been - Petrie and Breasted met in the late 1890s in Egypt, and although they got along quite well and were both primary Egyptologists from their home countries, they never worked together, something Petrie suggested they do so (Drower 1995, 217-8). The reason for this was that American archaeology and Egyptology were beginning to establish their own identities by the turn of the century. Breasted persuaded American tycoon J.D. Rockefeller to donate a large sum of money to the University of Chicago as an endowment to create the Oriental Exploration Society (OES). The OES became the Americans' primary Near Eastern archaeological organization, which meant they were no longer reliant on the English (Drower 1995, 286).

As Petrie's fame and success as an archeologist grew, so, too, did his social circle, which came to include a number of famous people outside of the realms of archaeology and Egyptology. While Petrie was living in the quiet London neighborhood of Bromley at the turn of the century, a curious Russian immigrant moved in next door to him in 1901. He was an older, fairly well-educated, and intelligent gentlemen whom Petrie immediately liked. Petrie was later a bit surprised to learn that his new Russian neighbor was the intellectual and activist Peter Kropotkin. Beyond the books and pamphlets he wrote extolling the virtues of anarchism and the evils of monarchy, Kropotkin was famous for being imprisoned for his political activities, escaping prison in 1876, and fleeing to England in exile. He ended up in London, as many political exiles of the era did, living next door to the politically conservative Petrie. Although Petrie disagreed with Kropotkin's politics, he enjoyed the man's company and found him truly interesting (Drower 1995, 298).

Kropotkin

When World War I broke out in 1914, it put Petrie's excavations on hiatus, but it allowed him to get caught up on his publications. The war also allowed him to meet two men who would play a significant role during and after the war. During World War I, Tomas Masaryk was an ethnic Czech professor and activist who lived in the Austria-Hungarian Empire. His politics made him an enemy of his government, so he fled with his daughter and two students and ended up for a time in London, which is where he met Petrie and his family. Although Masaryk would leave London, two of his female students stayed behind to live with Petrie and his family for the remainder of the war. Masaryk would maintain his friendship with the Petrie family after the war, and in time he became the first President of Czechoslovakia (Drower 1995, 341).

Perhaps the most famous person Petrie met during World War I was one of the people who least impressed him. T.E. Lawrence, better known as Lawrence of Arabia, helped organize Arab resistance to the Ottoman forces during World War I. Lawrence worked with British intelligence, funding and organizing the army of Hussein, the Grand Sharif of Mecca, which was fundamental in aiding the British forces at Damascus on September 30, 1918 (Hull and Jotischky 2009, 126-7).

Long before Lawrence was a spy and guerilla leader, he was an aspiring archaeologist. Petrie was leading his last excavation season in the Fayum in 1913-1914 when he met Lawrence. Although Petrie believed, as did many in Europe in late 1913 and early 1914, that war was probably inevitable, he continued with work as usual, which meant conducting excavations and hiring new students. When Petrie first met Lawrence, he was initially impressed with the young man's knowledge of Arabic, so he hired him (Drower 1995, 319). Once Lawrence began working, however, it was clear to Petrie that he did not share his love of archaeology. One morning, when Lawrence showed up to work in a blazer and soccer shorts, Petrie took a long look at the young man and said dryly, "We don't play cricket here" (Drower 1995, 320). Lawrence worked with Petrie for six weeks before going to Arabia to leave his mark on the world.

Lawrence of Arabia

The final chapter of Petrie's life would play out in Palestine, which was certainly an interesting place in his day. Today, much of what was called Palestine at the time is now Israel, but when Petrie lived there, it was part of the League of Nations' "mandate" system, which meant it was governed by Great Britain. The population was overwhelmingly Muslim, but there were a scattering of Christians and an ever-growing Jewish population. Although Arabic was the primary language of Palestine, Petrie found that the social and political situation was quite different, which made for some exciting and at times dangerous incidents.

Petrie first worked in Palestine during the 1889-90 season. There was plenty of work to be had in Palestine, especially for a Bible enthusiast like Petrie, but most of his work there focused on

Bronze Age sites with Egyptian influences. Not long after he arrived in Palestine, Petrie discovered it to be much more dangerous than Egypt. Once one had left the relatively safe confines of Jerusalem's walls, the hills around the city and desert to the south were essentially no man's lands, populated by thieves, bandits, and violent Bedouins. Petrie carried a gun for the first time in his travels due to security issues and the need to scare intruders and potential thieves from dig sites (Drower 1995, 159).

In Palestine, he also had to deal with a different bureaucracy. Until the end of World War I, Palestine was a part of the Ottoman Empire, which meant he had to deal with Turks coming from a system as ossified and more corrupt than the British system to which he was used in Egypt (Drower 1995, 164). After he was ambushed and robbed in his first season (Drower 1995, 164), Petrie settled in and eventually came to enjoy Palestine. He developed many business contacts throughout the country, and things became easier after control had passed from the Ottomans to the British. Petrie also enjoyed the climate and decided to retire there.

After Petrie retired to Jerusalem, he remained quite active, taking daily walks, writing, and giving lectures at local historical societies whenever he was up to it. With Hilda at his side, Petrie began working on a sort of memoir, titled *Seventy Years in Archaeology*, which was published in 1931. Since the book did not delve much into his personal life, it cannot be considered a true memoir, but it did reveal much about Petrie's thoughts on archaeology and Egyptology when he began, and where he thought the disciplines were headed in the future (Shaw and Nicholson 1995, 222). The book was read by those in the field and helped to increase his status in his final years. Petrie and his wife were often visited at their apartment by scholars from around the world, and they were always happy to entertain as best they could.

Petrie's last dig season was in 1937-38 in Tell el 'Ajjul in Palestine (Drower 1995, 470). Although his mind was still fairly sharp, he was growing frail and needed help. He kept up with current events and was worried see that Europe would soon be embroiled in another war, so it was somewhat ironic that Petrie and Hilda were relieved when they learned the Germans had captured their son because they knew that he would likely not be involved in combat for the remainder of the war (Drower 1995, 420).

Petrie was initially admitted to the hospital in late 1940 after a bout of malaria. Though the illness passed, it left him unable to walk. Petrie was given therapy when it became apparent that he was wasting away, but there was no real hope of him making a full recovery. The therapy continued in an effort to make his death comfortable. Hilda was with Petrie every day, but due to the war, Ann was unable to make the journey. She learned of the circumstances surrounding her father's death later in a telegram.

Petrie died relatively peacefully on July 28, 1942 in a Jerusalem hospital at the age of 89 and was buried in the Protestant cemetery on Mount Zion (Drower 1995, 423).

When he died in 1942, the great Sir William Flinders Petrie bequeathed several things to the world. When admitted to the hospital in late 1940, Petrie requested that if he should die, the Royal College of Surgeons in London preserve his skull for scientific study. The request was not considered strange at the time, and more than one doctor showed enthusiasm for the request.

They believed they would learn a lot by studying the brain of a man with such an incredible memory and intellectual talent, but the logistics of the war thwarted the plan. As it turned out, Petrie's head was mislabeled when it made back to England after the war ended, and it sat in a warehouse until the 1970s (Drower 1995, 424).

Of course, Petrie's greatest gifts to the world were the number of firsts he brought to the studies of archaeology and Egyptology, especially the scientific way in which he conducted excavations. Although Petrie's incredible discoveries were due to his great mind, his physical endurance and longevity in the field cannot be overlooked. He conducted excavations in Egypt almost every season for 40 years and in Palestine for several more in a career spanning nearly 70 years. Needless to say, that's a number that will be hard to surpass.

Egyptology in Petrie's time was cliquey, not to mention home to ambitious individuals who tossed people aside to get ahead, some of them with slight to extreme colonialist feelings who often viewed native Egyptians as inferior and only good for manual labor on excavation sites. Although Petrie did not always get along with everyone in the field, he was never vindictive and rarely harbored grudges, even when wronged. When it came to the native Egyptians, his views were mixed, somewhat paternalistic, and more enlightened than most of his contemporaries. Petrie's brand of Christianity was austere and certainly Protestant which, in many ways, helped prepare him for life in Egypt, living and working with the Egyptians. As discussed earlier, he lived in tombs during his first season in Egypt, and even after that, his living conditions improved very little. While many of his European and American colleagues stayed in hotels and apartments, Petrie preferred to live in tents and hastily built shacks, just like his Egyptian workers (Reid 2002, 176). Though his friends and colleagues often invited him to stay in nicer lodgings while in Egypt, which he would accept if traveling, he stayed with the Egyptian workers while in the field. He once told a friend, "All Arabs are my friends and I know them all." (Drower 1995, 50).

In addition to living among the Egyptians, Petrie made it a point to learn something about them and their culture. Throughout his life in Egypt, Petrie and later his wife became conversant in Arabic and followed modern Egyptian customs when around his workmen. He paid his workers better than most Europeans did and never resorted to beatings or other martial punishments if his men stepped out of line. In his writing, Petrie sometimes contrasted his respect for modern Egyptians with what he considered a lack of respect by many of his friends and colleagues. He wrote about one friend in particular, "He thinks the Arabs ought to learn somewhat of our manners when they deal with us, whereas I always take them on their own basis. He has no approximation to the easy-going, off-hand, joking, rub-shoulders way that softens the inexorableness of laying down the lay. If kind—as he wishes to be—there is so much condescension and superiority in his tone that I—as an Arab—should feel ribbed." (Drower 1995, 155).

Although Petrie's view of modern Egyptians appears socially liberal by the early 20th century's standards, it would be safer to consider it nuanced. On numerous occasions, he remarked and wrote that he found it difficult to believe that modern Egyptians, with their poverty and what he considered superstitions, could have descended from the ancient Egyptians, the builders of the world's first true civilization. Always searching for answers, Petrie thought he had found the answer to this dilemma in the Copts, Egypt's Christian minority, which comprised about 10% of the population. He believed the Copts to be more enlightened than their Muslim neighbors, once stating, "Egypt will never be a civilized land till it is ruled by the Copts—if ever." (Horbury 2011, 162).

Petrie's relationships were generally positive with the Western scholars living in Egypt and Egyptologists in general. Many Westerners thought Petrie was a little eccentric and quirky, but as his career progressed, it was inevitable that he would rub a few people the wrong way, and there were always those who were jealous of his success.

The professional conflicts Petrie had with other Egyptologists were usually ephemeral, but there was a notable one that lasted for his entire life. Wallis Budge was an eminent Egyptologist and curator of the Department of Egyptian and Assyrian Antiquities of the British Museum in the early 20th century, and the two men were initially cordial and appeared to be forging a professional relationship, but when Petrie learned that Budge had called the pottery he brought back from Egypt "worthless," it marked the beginning of a professional and personal grudge between the men (Drower 1995, 105). The fact that Budge was more established in Egyptology at the time and Petrie was essentially an upstart might have played a role in the conflict, but there is little doubt that Budge thought the pottery worthless. In the 19th century, archaeologists were still after big statues and monuments and not pottery. Petrie may have been ahead of the times in his collection of pottery, but it was hard for Budge, whose focus was language and religion, to realize that.

Personal and professional disagreements with the antiquities council in Egypt eventually drove Petrie to Palestine in his later career and life. For Petrie's first several decades in Egypt, there was an "equal shares" agreement whereby the antiquities council took half of all finds and decided which pieces would be kept in Egypt. The system worked well, allowing museums around the world to stock their shelves with ancient Egyptian antiquities. The agreement came to an end when Carter discovered King Tutankhamun's tomb in 1922. From that time on, it was nearly impossible for non-Egyptians to remove antiquities from Egypt, which was part of the reason Petrie went to Palestine (Jeffreys 2011, 11).

Despite blazing many archaeological and academic trails and changing the way Egyptology is studied, Petrie also made plenty of mistakes along the way, but he never seemed to have a problem admitting when he was wrong. Petrie was a true intellectual in that respect, learning from the mistakes he made and never treating them as failures.

A perfect example of Petrie's ability to learn from his mistakes is how quickly he changed his opinion of the "pyramid inch" after surveying the Great Pyramid of Giza. Once he knew Taylor and Smyth's theories about the Great Pyramid were wrong, he simply accepted that and moved on with more serious academic studies. This was also the case with initial excavations of the necropolis at Naqada. The site is now known to be a pre-dynastic necropolis, but when Petrie first excavated, he dated it to the First Intermediate Period (ca. 2125-1975 BCE) and theorized that the inhabitants had been a foreign ethnic group. Petrie held firmly to that opinion for many years, but once the necropolis proved to be an Egyptian pre-dynastic site, he accepted the findings without reservation (Drower 1995, 215).

Petrie's initial theory about Naqada revealed one of his primary faults as an Egyptologist: his problem with chronology. One might think that since Petrie was so accurate in his periodization of artifacts that he would have been quite skilled at determining chronology, but he was often way off in that regard. Petrie had an incredible ability to group his discoveries by periods, but when he looked at the "big picture" of centuries and millennia, he often fell far short of what is now known. Petrie's survey of ancient Egypt history, *A History of Egypt*, was published in several volumes in the early 20th century and is often compared to American Egyptologist James Henry Breasted's *History of Egypt*, published around the same time. Although Petrie's treatment of ancient Egyptian culture, religion, and historical events are for the most part accurate, his chronology was far off from Breasted's and what is now generally accepted. Petrie believed the Egyptian state had formed around the year 5546 BCE, while Breasted put it at 3400 BCE. Estimates today range from between 3100 and 2900 BCE (Drower 1995, 315).

Petrie made a few other minor mistakes over the course of his otherwise illustrious archaeology career. He continued to be interested in British archaeology for most of his life and sometimes lectured on findings and theories pertaining to the subject. Petrie had a special place in his heart for pre-Roman British archaeology, as evidenced by his work at Stonehenge and Silbury Hill. For most of his life, Petrie argued Stonehenge to be the burial location of ancient Celtic kings, which has since been proven incorrect (Drower 1995, 350).

To be fair, his wrong presumptions about Stonehenge are mitigated by the fact that he was an Egyptologist first, but he did have a definite weakness when it came to ancient Egyptian archaeology. Most of Petrie's major discoveries in ancient Egypt were either in necropolises or some other site in a funerary context, such as pyramids and other tombs, reflective of the fact that like most Egyptologists of the period, Petrie believed the way to truly understand ancient Egyptian history was to uncover it from the top down, beginning with the kings, nobles, and high-priests. Thanks to this philosophy, Petrie often overlooked settlements which might have revealed plenty of details about how most ancient Egyptians lived. Jeffreys noted, "Despite Petrie's formidable reputation, it is also worth remembering that his strengths and those of many of his contemporaries were in cemetery archaeology; almost all their settlement excavations were poorly conducted, even by the standards of the times. In some ways Egypt, particularly the Nile Delta, was regarded as an accessory to biblical archaeology…in the same way that, if included at all, it had been the last leg of the traditional route for visits to the Holy Land as part of the Grand Tour from the 18th to the earlier part of the 19th century." (Jeffreys 2011, 9).

As with all academics, the key to staying relevant is publication, which is why Petrie published so many titles. He did receive some criticism from some of his contemporaries, who were critical of him for condensing his notes rather than publishing detailed field notes. In fact, most of the original notes from his digs were lost (Shaw and Nicholson 1995, 222). Petrie did, however, know what those in the academic community looked for as far as relevant publications were concerned, which is partially why he embarked on publishing a journal titled *Ancient Egypt*. The journal was meant to compete with the E.E.S.'s *Journal of Egyptian Archaeology* (JEA), but AE has been defunct for several decades while JEA is the premier English language Egyptology journal (Drower 1995, 327).

Of course, Petrie's mistakes pale in comparison when placed in the context of his full career. If anything, Petrie continues to be one of the driving forces behind a field that continues to thrive today.

Howard Carter and Tutankhamun's Tomb

Howard Carter

Howard Carter was born on May 9, 1874 in London, the the son of the relatively successful artist Samuel John Carter. Howard inherited his father's artistic talents, and it was this which eventually led him to a career in Egyptology.

During his teens he became acquainted with the Egyptologist P.E. Newberry, and in the autumn of 1891, when he was only 17, Carter was hired to work as a copyist with Newberry at Beni Hassan and Deir el-Bersha in Egypt, making copies of inscriptions found on tomb and temple walls. Thus began Carter's career in Egyptology.

His work as a copyist quickly progressed, and from 1893-1899 he became responsible for copying the inscriptions and scenes found on the walls of the Queen Hatshepsut's temple at Deir el-Bahri. Carter's career progressed even further when he was appointed Chief Inspector of Antiquities of the Upper Egypt region, which historically corresponds to everything south of the Nile delta, with Lower Egypt referring to the Delta region itself. The distinction is geographical rather than polar; southern Egypt (Upper Egypt) is of a higher elevation than Lower Egypt is. These designations were defined by the Ancient Egyptians themselves and are still followed today by many historians. Occasionally one may find mention of a Middle Egypt region, a more modern construct used to simplify Egypt's regions. As its name implies, it refers to the middle area of Egypt, roughly outlining the area from Memphis down to Asyut. In 1904 Carter changed posts from that of Chief Inspector of Antiquities of Upper Egypt, to Chief Inspector of Lower Egypt, making him responsible for the archaeological sites in the Delta.

It was during his time as Chief Inspector for Lower Egypt that Carter became indirectly embroiled in the situation which would bring to a close his career with the Antiquities service, and which would in turn lead him to the employment of the Earl of Carnarvon. In 1904, an incident arose that involved a party of European visitors and the Antiquities Services' Egyptian employees. Carter's unwavering support for his Egyptian workers in a time when equality between classes and cultures was a rare occurrence was ill regarded by his contemporaries and resulted in him leaving the Antiquities Service a year later in 1905. From 1905-1909 Carter occupied his time with odd jobs offering his services as an artist to individuals or as a draftsman and copyist to other archaeologists.

It was in 1909 that Carter began his association and partnership with Lord Carnarvon. Carnarvon had first come to Egypt in 1905 for his health after he had been injured in a car accident, and he soon became enamored of Egyptian archaeology. He had wished to fund some excavations himself, but he was told by the Antiquities Service that he must work with an experienced archaeologist before they would give him leave to excavate. This made Carter a natural partner, since Carter was a skilled and knowledgeable excavator with both the time and the inclination to form a new partnership. The two men soon gained permission to excavate and began working at Asasif, located in the Theban necropolis. Although the pair were keen to work in the Valley of the Kings, they instead found themselves working at various other sites, some even as far off as the Delta, while waiting for permission to excavate in the Valley of the Kings. The American archaeologist Theodore M. Davis had already been granted permission to work in the Valley of the Kings, and it was not until he retired in 1914 that Carter and Carnarvon were finally granted rights to the Valley of the Kings.

It would be another 8 years before the pair made their discovery of Tutankhamun's tomb. Perhaps unsurprisingly, those eight years of what they considered mediocre discoveries and false trails left Carnarvon frustrated and ready to give up the quest of finding a royal tomb. But Carter persevered and managed to convince Carnarvon to fund one last season, and thus the dig season of 1922-23 commenced. The traditional dig season for Egypt was from November to March, because Egypt's hot climate made it best to dig during the cooler months of winter.

Carter and Carnarvon's excavation that year began near the tomb of Ramesses VI, a somewhat unusual location as it was in line with a water runoff. Such an area would have been filled with sand and rubble that had been dumped there from the rain water running down the mountain side.   As it turned out, Carter chose just the right spot. On November 4, 1922, only a few days into the season, what looked to be the entrance to an as yet unknown tomb was discovered. This initial indication of a tomb was nothing more than a step cut into the bedrock of the valley floor. The next day further digging revealed a staircase that led down to a blocked doorway. The stones blocking the doorway were plastered over with mud and covered in seal impressions bearing marks of the necropolis, though at the time no royal name could be discerned. Lord Carnarvon was away in England at the time of the discovery, so Carter re-filled the stairway with rubble and sent a telegram to Carnarvon notifying him of the discovery: "At last made wonderful discovery in Valley; a magnificent tomb with seals intact; recovered same for your arrival; congratulations." With that, Carter awaited his return.

The site of Tutankhamun's tomb. Picture by Peter J. Bubenik

Carter also contacted a friend and colleague, Arthur Callender, to help with the excavation on the tomb. Upon the return of Lord Carnarvon to Gurna, the housing quarters of Carter and some of his team, the team started working again on November 23, with Callender clearing the stairway in one day. That revealed more seals upon the entrance of the tomb, including one bearing the cartouche of Tutankhamun. Exciting as this discovery was, it was soon hampered by the realization that the tomb doorway had been re-opened and closed again at some point in the ancient past, usually a strong indication that a tomb had been robbed in antiquity. Nonetheless, the discovery of what would prove to be a new royal tomb was truly exciting.

Once the stone covering the doorway had been removed, a descending corridor filled with rubble was revealed and soon cleared. It took two days to do this, and on the afternoon of Sunday, November 26, a second sealed doorway was found. As with the first doorway, it too was covered with seals bearing the cartouche of Tutankhamun. Due to their excitement over this discovery, the group decided to make a small opening in the top left corner of the doorway, and they then inserted a candle through the opening of the tomb to reveal what was inside. In Carter's own words, taken from his journal, this is what he saw:

'It was sometime before one could see, the hot air escaping caused the candle to flicker, but as soon as one's eyes became accustomed to the glimmer of light the interior of the chamber gradually loomed before one, with its strange and wonderful medley of extraordinary and beautiful objects heaped upon one another.

There was naturally short suspense for those present who could not see, when Lord Carnarvon said to me 'Can you see anything. I replied to him 'Yes, it is wonderful'. I then with precaution made the hole sufficiently large for both of us to see. With the light of an electric torch as well as an additional candle we looked in. Our sensations and astonishment are difficult to describe as the better light revealed to us the marvellous collection of treasures: two strange ebony-black effigies of a King, gold sandalled, bearing staff and mace, loomed out from the cloak of darkness; gilded couches in strange forms, lion-headed, Hathor-headed, and beast infernal; exquisitely painted, inlaid and ornamental caskets; flowers; alabaster vases, some beautifully executed of lotus and papyrus device; strange black shrines with a gilded monster snake appearing from within; quite ordinary looking white chests; finely carved chairs; a golden inlaid throne; a heap of large curious white oviform boxes; beneath our very eyes, on the threshold, a lovely lotiform wishing-cup in translucent alabaster; stools of all shapes and design, of both common and rare materials; and lastly a confusion of overturned parts of chariots glinting with gold, peering from amongst which was a manikin. The first impression of which suggested the property-room of an opera of a vanished civilization. Our sensations were bewildering and full of strange emotion."

A pectoral belonging to Tutankhamun, representing his Prenomen.

Howard Carter and Lord Carnarvon had just made the archaeological find of the century, and one that has yet to be surpassed by any other Egyptologists. Excavation would continue to be carried out by an expert team of photographers, draftsmen, conservationists and so forth, in a detailed and meticulous manner: Arthur Callender, engineer; Arthur Mace, archaeologist, curator and conservationist; Harry Burton, archaeologist and photographer; Alfred Lucas, chemist, conservationist; Sir Alan Gardiner, Egyptologist and philologist; James Henry Breasted, Egyptologist; Percy Newberry, Egyptologist and botanist; Essie Newberry, conservationist; Douglas Derry, anatomist (and the first to examine the body of Tutankhamun); Lindsey Hall, draughtsman; Walter Hauser, archaeologist and architect. These men and women were just a few of those who worked on uncovering the secrets of Tutankhamun and his tomb, not to mention the many Egyptian workmen, and their Reis Ahmed, and Hussein Abou Omar. The death of Lord Carnarvon on April 5, 1923 neither paused nor halted the recoding and removal of the objects found in Tutankhamun's tomb.

The West Valley tomb of the young King Tutankhamun is not the greatest of all the tombs in Ancient Egypt. It's not the greatest of all the tombs in the Valley of the Kings; in fact, the pharaoh affectionately known to most of the world as "King Tut" was not even one of Ancient Egypt's most powerful rulers. Still, King Tut's Valley tomb is exceptional in that, unlike nearly all other tombs in Ancient Egypt, it was found almost entirely intact. The small tomb of this relatively unimportant ruler contained a vast fortune of nearly 3,500 treasures, thus offering some perspective on the tombs that were largely empty upon their discoveries. If one considers the great wealth which adorned the tomb of such a minor king, it becomes possible—though only scarcely—to imagine the treasures which must have been contained within the tombs of greater New Kingdom pharaohs.

It is important to remember that there was much more to the objects found in Tutankhamun's tomb than just affirming his position as Egypt's ruler. All the 5,398 objects recovered from his tomb had a purpose and a role to play in helping Tutankhamun on his journey into and through the afterlife. While we may never know the exact purpose of every single object, we do know that there would have been a purpose, and the majority of the objects can roughly be divided into a few main groups.

In addition to objects meant to preserve the body and mummy, one category of objects consists of those that were intended to help Tutankhamun in the afterlife, to keep him safe and to help maintain his identity. With the increasing importance that was placed upon the god Osiris, one's afterlife became centered on the journey through the underworld. The king would have followed the sun god on his path through the underworld at night and be reborn with him in the morning with the sun rise. Many of the objects found in Tutankhamun's tomb were intended to safeguard him on the journey through the underworld. Objects such as magical figurines, amulets, images of deities, and even the paintings on the wall were there to help the king in the afterlife, while other objects such as crocks and flails were symbols of Tutankhamun's status. The king needed to retain his royal status in the afterlife. The crock and the flail were ancient symbols of Egyptian kingship, as were the serpent and vulture headed uraei on his funerary mask and the depiction of him standing triumphant over the enemies of Egypt. All of these were representations of Tutankhamun's status as a king of Egypt.

Another category to be considered is that of daily life. Thousands of the objects found in the tomb, ranging from the piles of food, clothing, furniture, chariots, and weapons were reminders of the life Tutankhamun had lived, and they were placed there so that he might carry them with him into his afterlife. Some of the objects were symbols of what he had in life, such as that of the shabti figurines, which were made to look like people. These figurines, with some of them performing certain tasks and others standing still, were meant to represent the servants that Tutankhamun had possessed in life and the continued service and help that they would offer him in the afterlife. The food was meant to be a reminder of what he had eaten in life and to provide nourishment in the afterlife.

Although most of the objects have a clearly identifiable purpose, that of preservation, protection, or representation, others do not. For example, there are three large ornate couches that are something of a curiosity. It has been determined that they were custom made for the king's burial, so they were not objects that had previously been used while he was alive. While they must have been intended in some way to be of use to the king in his afterlife, their specific purpose is not known. If they had been meant to represent objects the king had used during his life, it's unclear why these were purposely built for his afterlife as opposed to placing couches he had used in life in the tomb.

Regardless of the purposes and mysteries of the objects, the scope, detail, and craftsmanship of the thousands of objects in Tutankhamun's tomb are magnificent, and the discovery of the relatively unspoiled tomb was and is every archaeologist's dream. But what did the tomb and its objects actually provide that was not already known? The tomb itself was small, and architectural and artistically it was and is a poor example of New Kingdom royal tombs. It offered no new information except to imply that the king buried within it must have died unexpectedly and before his own tomb had been completed. The objects found within the tomb, while amazing, held very little historical value. From many other tomb drawings, painting, and artifacts, Egyptologist already had a firm understanding of what everyday life was like in Ancient Egypt, as well as knowledge of the religious practices and the burial practices. Thus, the tomb and its objects provided very little information concerning the life of Tutankhamun; in essence, all they really provided was a confirmation of the identity of the mummy.

A golden shrine found in the tomb

Frank Rytell's picture of an alabaster jar found in the tomb

John Campana's picture of a wooden chest found in the tomb

Ever since it was discovered that the mummy of Tutankhamun was that of an adolescent, the cause of his demise has been shrouded in mystery. What caused an 18 or 19 year old boy to die, especially when that boy had been raised in a royal court with the best foods, education, and doctors available to him? It was postulated by some that he was murdered as part of some sort of political coup. Others thought he must have been sickly and died as the result of some genetic disease or deformity.

For decades, very little light could be shed upon the cause of his death. However, with the advent of modern medical technology it recently became possible to subject his mummy to a number of scans, including CT scans, and DNA analysis. CT scans showed that not long before he had died, he had suffered a severely broken leg, followed by an infection. This evidence, coupled with the presence of malaria in his system (revealed by the DNA scans), combine to give a very plausible cause of death. It is very likely that Tutankhamun died of illness that was the result of the infection in his leg and malaria. Such illness would have easily brought about an unexpected and sudden death, and the very nature of Tutankhamun's tomb and burial support the notion that his death had been unexpected.

In terms of its design, King Tut's tomb was not so interesting as most other tombs in the Valley, doubtless due to Tutankhamun's death at a young age. The tomb of Tutankhamun, KV62, is very small, especially by New Kingdom royal tomb standards. It consists of a sloping corridor that leads down to four small rooms or chambers. The plan of the tomb is very different from that of earlier 18th dynasty rulers; indeed, its small size, cramped rooms, and unusual design imply that it had originally been intended for use by a nobleman, not the king. With Tutankhamun's unexpected death, he was probably placed into the smaller tomb because his own was not completed or ready to receive a burial. The decoration found on the walls of the tomb was most likely painted on between the time of his death and burial. Though abbreviated, the decoration was still of a very traditional nature, and the condensed scenes would have been due to the lack of appropriate space.

Tut's tomb consisted of an entrance which leads to a single corridor. This was followed by several annexes meant to contain Tut's funerary equipment. At a 90 degree right angle from the tomb's corridor was Tut's modest burial chamber, which featured another annex that leads back towards the direction of the entrance. Only the burial chamber of the tomb was decorated. All of the walls featured the same golden background. The west wall was covered with scenes depicting the *apes* of the first hour of the Amduat. On the south wall, King Tut was followed by Anubis as he appeared before Hathor, and another scene on this wall showed King Tut as he was welcomed into the underworld by Anubis, Hathor, and Isis. On the north wall, King Tut is depicted with the royal *ka* before the goddess Nut as he embraces Osiris. The same wall showed Tut's successor, Ay, as he performs the Opening of the Mouth ritual before the mummified Tutankhamun. On the east wall, those in the funerary procession are depicted as they pull King Tut's mummy on a sledge.

Despite the return to more traditional burial practices, there were still vestiges of the Amarna period to be found. Some of the figures of the king and of the deities retained the same canonical proportions seen during the Amarna period. It is unlikely that this was meant to make any deliberate statement concerning his lineage or religious preference, but was instead the result of multiple artists being used to decorate the tomb.

Upon entering the burial chamber, excavators were met with what seemed to be a wall of gilded wood which featured an inlay of glittering blue faience. This "wall" was the outermost shrine in the group of nested shrines by which the pharaoh's sarcophagus was protected. These shrines were carefully built constructions made mostly of cedar and held together by tendons of bronze, oak, and wood. Within the outermost shrine were contained a pall frame, a second, third, and fourth inner shrine, and, finally the sarcophagus itself. Each of these shrines was bound with copper on its lower edge, and each eastern end featured a set of double folding doors. These doors were held shut by ebony bolts which slid within giant, silver-coated staples. Each door also had two additional staples which were intended to receive a cord binding and seal.

A picture of Howard Carter opening shrine doors in the tomb

A picture of the seal on the tomb

The first shrine bore a striking resemblance to the sed-festival pavilion in which the pharaoh was believed to achieve rejuvenation and rebirth. It was constructed of heavy cedar panels, each of which were gessoed, gilded, and inlaid on both their insides and their outsides. The rear and side panels of the outermost shrine were decorated with knot amulets of Isis and the hieroglyphs of Osiris—these were set against a striking blue faience background. A pair of protective Wadjet eyes adorned the southern side of the shrine, and each of the shrine's doors was adorned with a rectangular panel that contained sunken reliefs. The relief on the left depicted a headless and lawless lion-like creature, while the relief on the right featured a seated divinity who was wearing a twin feather headdress and grasping an ankh, which was the sign of life. On the inside surfaces, the outermost shrine was inscribed with extracts from the Book of the Dead—spells 1, 134, 141, and 142—[34]as well as extracts from the Book of the Heavenly Cow. The inside of the roof of the outermost shrine was decorated with 13 vultures and a number of winged solar disks.

The second shrine was made up of 16 heavy, wooden sections, most of which had been gessoed and gilded with a layer of gold leaf. The roof of the second shrine was covered with thick, black resin which was divided into squares by gilded bands of incised decorations. Each door's exterior surface was adorned with a sublime sunken relief depiction of Tutankhamun as he stood before Osiris and Re-Horakhty. At the shrine's rear stood Nephthys and Isis, the sisters

---

[34] "Here begin the spells of going out into the day, the praises and recitations for going to and fro in the realm of the dead which are beneficial in the beautiful West, and which are to be spoken on the day of burial and of going in after going out"—Book of the Dead, spell 1.

of Osiris and the principal mourners at the funeral of the deified pharaoh. The rest of the outside of the second shrine was decorated with an assortment of texts and vignettes from a number of funerary compositions, including the Book of the Dead, as well as with its own unique cryptographic funerary book having to do with the triumph of light.

On its interior, this ceiling of the second shrine featured a figure of the winged goddess Nut which surmounted the hieroglyph for "gold"; these were accompanied by five vultures with their wings outstretched. On either side of Nut were engraved spells from both the Pyramid Texts and the Book of the Dead. On the inside surface of the right door was depicted a donkey-headed messenger alongside the ram-headed guardian of the underworld; the left door featured a similar depiction of an underworld guardian standing beside a human-headed figure. Above the images on either door was the text from spell 144 of the Book of the Dead.[35] The right and left panels of the second shrine featured sunken relief vignettes from the Book of the Dead. The right side depicted seven celestial cows, the bull of heaven, and the four udders of heaven (spell 148), while the left side depicted spells 141 and 142[36] along with the text of spells 130, 133, 134, and 148. The rear panel of the shrine was inscribed with spell 17 of the Book of the Dead, a statement of the solar doctrine in which the deceased Tutankhamun was identified with the creator-god.

The third outer shrine was made of up 10 separate sections; like the first shrine, it was gilded with gold leaf and strikingly decorated with sunken reliefs depicting vignettes from a number of Egyptian funerary texts. On the roof of the third shrine was a winged solar disc and a row of eight birds with their wings outstretched—these included four vultures, two serpent-headed vultures, and two falcons. On the sides of the shrine was depicted an abridged version of the second and sixth divisions of the Book of What is in the Underworld. The rear of the shrine and its outer doors both featured extracts from spell 148 of the Book of the Dead;[37] this text was

---

[35] "O you gates, you who keep the gates because of Osiris, O you who guard them and who report the affairs of the Two Lands to Osiris every day; I know you and I know your names..." The deceased had to know the names of the creatures which guarded each of the seven gates of the underworld in order to be able to persuade them to let him pass through.

[36] Used by the deceased to praise the gods upon entering their presence, these spells vindicated the worthiness of the deceased to be admitted into the presence of the gods and allow him to take his rightful place among them as a "vindicated soul" in the afterlife.

[37] 'For making provision for a spirit in the realm of the dead'. This spell provided the names of the Bull of Heaven and his seven cows, providing an eternal supply of food and beer. Their names are:

The names of the cattle are:
Mansion of Kas, Mistress of All.

Silent One who dwells in her place
She of Chemmis whom the god ennobled
The Much Beloved, red of hair
She who protects in life, the particolored.
She whose name has power in her craft.
Storm in the sky which wafts the god aloft
The bull, husband of the cows.

adorned with four ram-headed guardian figures and four messengers, each of whom grips one or two knives. The top of the third shrine was decorated similarly, featuring featured a winged disc, five vultures, a serpent-headed vulture, a sixth vulture, and a falcon. On the inner walls of the shrine are depicted the progressions of various gods, while the inner doorways specifically show Isis and Nephthys with their wings outstretched in order to protect King Tutankhamun.

The innermost shine consisted of only five separate sections and is believed to be a miniature reconstruction of the Palace of the North. Its barrel-vaulted roof was decorated with a bas relief depicting kneeling figures of Isis, Nephthys, Neith, and Selkis. These figures are alternated with Wadjet-eyes, recumbent Anubis dogs, and vultures. The reliefs on the left and right panels depict a procession of Imsety, Anubis, Duamutef, Hapy, Geb, Horus, and Qebhsenuef. On the end panel and outside door panels, Isis and Nepthys were once again seen protecting the pharaoh on his way to the underworld. The ceiling of this innermost shrine features a striking representation of the goddess Nut—also with her wings outstretched—flanked by a representation of Horus with a falcon head. Isis and Nephthys guard the inner doors still once more while the panels of the interior walls are inscribed with the text of spell 17 of the Book of the Dead.

Nestled inside these four spectacular shrines was the sarcophagus which contained the mummy of King Tutankhamun. This sarcophagus had a sloping lid and was engraved with a winged sun disk at its head. On its spine were three vertical columns of incised hieroglyphs. Both the sun disk and glyphs were made of red granite; however, they were painted yellow in order to match the sarcophagus box, which suggests that the lid was prepared hastily as a substitute for an original lid that was not ready upon the death of the king. As for the sarcophagus itself, its decorative theme featured the four tutelary deities—Isis, Nephthys, Selkis, and Neith, each carved in high relief and painted in vivid color. One of these deities stands at each corner of the sarcophagus box with their wings outstretched in a protective embrace. At its top edge, the sarcophagus box featured a cavetto cornice; at the bottom was a dado of double tyet and djed amulets. Each of the sarcophagus' long sides was decorated with seven columns of hieroglyphs and an inscribed Wadjet-eye. The short sides simply featured several bands of texts.

Despite the splendor and opulence of his funerary materials, nothing could compare to the treasures which adorned the mummy of King Tut. Attached to the mummy was a vast array of items intended to provide him with the protection he would need in order to pass into the Field of Reeds. Most are familiar, of course, with the gleaming golden mask that depicted the young king; however, an astonishing 106 other items were found attached to his mummy, both on its outside and within its bandages. One of the more significant of these items was a black resin scarab that hung suspended from the neck of the mummified King Tut on a golden band. The scarab was inscribed with spell 29b from the Book of the Dead.[38] Underneath this was a pair of burnished gold hands which were sewn directly onto the mummy wrappings. These hands clasped the decay crook and flail. Below these was a large gold ba-bird. As the wrappings of

---

[38] This spell guarded against the loss of the heart, by means of a heart amulet. It reads "I am the benu, the soul of Ra, who guides gods to the Netherworld when they go forth. The souls on earth will do what they desire, and the soul of [the deceased] will go forth at his desire."

Tutankhamun's mummy were removed, more and more of these elaborate treasures were revealed, among them were magnificent pieces of jewelry, magical amulets, and a number of other funerary objects, all fashioned and positioned according to the dictates of the Book of the Dead. All 107 treasures were meant to ensure that the pharaoh would be able to transcend death and take his rightful place among the gods in the Field of Reeds.

Detail from Tutankhamun's throne in the tomb

Reliefs in the tomb

A depiction of Nut in the tomb

The discovery of King Tut's tomb is the most exciting discovery that has been made to date in the Valley of the Kings. Elsewhere in the Valley, nearly all of the other royal tombs were robbed in antiquity. By the time a Greek historian visited the site in 60 BCE, he wrote that he found virtually nothing there "except the results of pillage and destruction."

Unfortunately, the world may never know what splendors lay within the Valley tombs of Egypt's most beloved pharaohs. However, it is not beyond the realm of possibility another tomb will be found that, like Tutankhamun's, escaped the notice of even the savviest ancient tomb robbers. Only time and further archaeological excavation will tell.

Uncovering Lost Cities

Although he is now one of the most visible and renowned archaeologists in the world, Franck Goddio's academic career began rather inauspiciously. Goddio grew up in France as a good scholar but entered higher education studying finance and economics, which is how he began his professional life working as a financial adviser. However, even while Goddio advised his clients about investments and made plenty of money doing so, he was always drawn to the ocean and the many secrets it held underneath. He began training in underwater archaeology in the mid-1980s and worked on several small excavations before earning the chance to undertake his first major dig in Egypt in 1992. That year, the Supreme Council of Antiquities, the Egyptian government organization that assigns all archaeological permits, offered Goddio the chance to excavate Alexandria's harbor (Adams 2008). Goddio's work uncovered numerous statues and smaller artifacts that dated to the time of the Ptolemies and Roman Egypt, cementing his reputation as an underwater archaeologist and solidifying his love of ancient Egyptian history.

After his work in Alexandria, Goddio traveled the world excavating sunken ships and other treasures across numerous underwater archaeological sites. He also founded the European Institute of Underwater Archaeology (EIUA) in 1987.

As Goddio explored shipwrecks around the world, an insatiable drive to rediscover Heracleion brought him back to Egypt in the mid-1990s, and ironically, it was one of the defining events of modern history that led Goddio to Heracleion's location. This is because when Goddio came to the region in the mid-1990s with an EIUA team to search for offshore remains, he was searching for remnants of the Napoleonic Wars, and it just so happened that the Battle of the Nile had been fought on the water close to where Heracleion sat on the seafloor.

Understandably, historians figured some artifacts might be located on sunken French ships, but in 1996, as EIUA underwater archaeologists searched for ships dating back to the end of the 18th century, they discovered stone slabs that were clearly much older. The archeologists who made the initial discovery could not read the writing on the slabs, but they knew they were looking at ancient Egyptian text. Goddio believed he had made an important discovery, so he assembled a team of 40 scholars, including Egyptologists who knew the ancient history of the region and would be able to read the inscriptions (Sooke 2016).

Not long after making the initial discovery, Goddio determined that he had found the remains of Heracleion, but the intrepid underwater archaeologist also knew full well that the excavation would be no easy task due to the size of the area and the geological features of the bay. The sandy bottom of the bay had consumed nearly everything, so almost nothing was visible on the seafloor, and even when Goddio and his divers made their way to the ruins of Heracleion, they could only see six inches in front of them due to the sandy bottom (Sooke 2016). This also means that whenever excavators attempt to recover a piece from the seafloor, of any size but especially larger objects, the sand is disturbed further reducing visibility. Due to the size of the city and the logistics of underwater archaeology, Goddio estimates that he has so far only uncovered about five percent of Heracleion (Sooke 206).

Despite only uncovering a small fraction of the overall site, what Goddio uncovered and brought to the surface was incredible. More than 150 feet below the water and four miles out in the sea, Goddio and his team discovered that the ruins of Heracleion encompassed an area of more than a mile, complete with the remains of temples, walls, large statues, and hundreds of smaller artifacts (Stanley and Toscano 2009, 164). Although Heracleion is not believed to have been as large as some of the other major ancient Egyptian cities such as Thebes or Memphis, the discovery also confirmed the classical accounts about Naucratis and Canopus. Armed with the knowledge that the cities essentially served as a large metropolitan port, Goddio could rightly assume that since his team had only partially uncovered what was already an impressive discovery, Heracleion must have been huge (Sooke 2016).

Goddio's finds indicate that the population of the city was densely packed into the series of islands, isthmuses, and peninsulas that made up Heracleion. Long, deep valleys on the seafloor show that the city was divided by a number of different canals and channels, all of which were used to ferry people and goods from the port to the Mediterranean Sea and the Canopic branch of the Nile River.

So far, most of the underwater excavations have focused on what was once an island that stood between the city's primary canal and a channel of the port basin. On this island once stood a structure that the Greek writers referred to as the Hercules Temple, but which was actually a temple dedicated to the Egyptian god Amun-Gereb. The Greeks referred to the god as Hercules out of a habit of equating Egypt's pantheon of gods with their own mythology, but in Egyptian religion and mythology Amun and all of his syncretic manifestations were associated with kingship, and he was the nation's preeminent god during the New Kingdom (Wilkinson 2003, 98-100). Thus, the Greeks saw him as a martial god much like Hercules.

Two colossal statues once stood at the entrance to the temple, greeting priests who went there for their daily rituals and travelers coming in and out of the city (Goddio 2018a). Visitors to the temple would have been brought there by the Grand Canal, which was the largest and most centrally located waterway in the city (Bomhard 2014, 342). The Grand Canal not only functioned as Heracleion's primary waterway, but also as the city's main street. In essence, ancient Heracleion would have looked very similar to Venice, with most traffic being conducted via boats on canals and other waterways. The densely packed population would have had to rely on marine transportation for the most part.

The significance of the Amun-Gereb Temple cannot be understated. It not only greeted all visitors to Heracleion, but also served as the center of the city's political power. The god Amun was one of the most important deities of ancient Egypt's New Kingdom and Late Period, so any temple dedicated to him was sure to be well-funded, and the priests of the cult wielded enormous power. Goddio himself noted, "It was the port of entry to Egypt, so all trade had to go through the city. Furthermore, it possessed a temple where every pharaoh had to go in order to receive the title of their power, as universal sovereign, from the supreme god Amun. So it was very wealthy." (Sooke 2016).

Ancient Egyptian temples were also places where significant economic activity was carried out. This made sense because temples took up significant amounts of agricultural land, making them logical places to serve as administrative centers (Shaw and Nicholson 1995, 286).

In addition to being the largest structure discovered at Heracleion so far, the Amun-Gereb Temple has also yielded the most in terms of artifacts. Hundreds of ceramic amulets and the remains of a wooden naos, which possibly held the cult statue of Amun-Gereb, have been discovered in what was once the foundation of the Amun-Gereb Temple (Bomhard 2014, 340). It was actually quite common in the Near East for people to place religiously significant artifacts or inscriptions in the foundation of a new or refurbished temple, so when archeologists find a foundation deposit cache, it can help them determine the date of the structure in question. Egyptologists who have had the opportunity to examine the finds from Heracleion, namely the artifacts discovered in the Amun-Gereb Temple, have determined that the temple is probably as old as the city, being built sometime in the 7th century BCE during the Twenty-Sixth Dynasty. With that said, some of the artifacts from the foundation deposits have been dated by art historians to the Thirtieth Dynasty and the Ptolemies, which means that the temple was also renovated in the 4th century BCE and possibly the 3rd century BCE (Bomhard 2014, 352).

There were over 300 amulets discovered in the foundation deposits, with some of the most interesting being small lead boats (Heinz 2011, 2012). Hundreds of small model boats have been discovered throughout Egypt, but unlike modern model boats, which serve as toys or decorations, ancient Egyptian model boats were for funerary and cult rituals (Shaw and Nicholson 1995, 269). In terms of funerary art, the Egyptians would often place model boats in tombs in order to help the deceased travel in the underworld. The other common context where model boats were often used was in religious rituals, particularly for carrying the sacred cult statue of a deity from one temple to another. It is believed that the model boats discovered in Heracleion were used in a ritual context to carry images of deities to other temples in the area, such as the one in Canopus (Heinz 2011, 218).

Aside from the religious context of the boat models discovered in the Amun-Gereb Temple foundation deposits, the people of Heracleion had a particular affinity for marine travel, the sea, and the Nile River, so it's possible that some of the models served other purposes. Before the 7th century BCE, marine travel was infrequent and sea vessels usually hugged the shoreline, but after coming into contact with the Greeks (which is when Heracleion was built), the Egyptians adopted better seagoing ships (Shaw and Nicholson 1995, 269). Thus, the Egyptians in Heracleion were much more connected to the sea and the Greek world than the rest of the country, and they were more influenced by foreigners and their ideas, having lived and worked next to them in Naucratis, Canopis, and their own harbor. It would be plausible that they began making some of the boat models purely for pleasure.

Heracleion's differences from the rest of Egypt would not have been immediately apparent to those coming to the city from the south. Visitors from other parts of Egypt would have been greeted by the Amun-Gereb Temple, which was purely Egyptian in its architectural style, but once in the city they would have heard different languages and seen customs not like theirs. Egyptians with an agricultural background who visited Heracleion regularly to use the markets, ports, or to make pilgrimages to the Amun-Gereb Temple, would have entered a cosmopolitan world that was vastly different than the one they lived in every day.

The Amun-Gereb Temple would have unified all Egyptians in the city, but despite the god's popularity among native Egyptians, who viewed the god as crucial to the city's existence, the Greek population probably did not participate much in the cult's activities (Heinz 2011, 222). The Greeks had their own gods and would have looked at the Egyptian gods with curiosity at best.

The Amun-Gereb Temple is the most impressive and important structure in Heracleion to have been excavated so far, but Goddio and his team uncovered other monuments that demonstrate the size and stature of the city. On the north end of Heracleion, there was a channel that once connected the different parts of the city and was appropriately named the North Channel. Next to the North Channel, Goddio and his team discovered a multilingual colossal stela dated to the reign of Ptolemy VIII (ruled 170-163 BCE and 145-116 BCE). The multilingual text was common for the era, echoing the more famous Rosetta Stone from the same period, as Egypt had by the 3rd century BCE become a country ruled by a non-Egyptian minority that assimilated Egyptian culture, especially outside of Alexandria. The stela's text, like most others of the era, was written in Greek, the Egyptian hieroglyphic script, and Egyptian demotic script, not only for various audiences (Goddio 2018a), but also as a way to let the native Egyptians know who ruled their country.

On an island located between the North Channel and Grand Canal, there was a sanctuary for the Egyptian god Khonsu-Thoth. Although not as big or as important as the Amun-Gereb Temple, the Khonsu-Thoth sanctuary's location in the city demonstrates that the people of Heracleion reserved a special place for this god. Khonsu was associated with the moon and important in later Egyptian history (Wilkinson 2003, 113), while Thoth, also known as Djehuty, was the ibis-headed god of wisdom, learning, and knowledge (Wilkinson 2003, 215). The sanctuary was located next to the port (Goddio 2018a), and as with the Amun-Gereb Temple, all mariners coming in and out of the city would have been greeted by the Khonsu-Thoth sanctuary.

Numerous other religious artifacts have also been uncovered but have yet to be studied very carefully. A pair of statues about 16 feet tall have been pulled from the sea, and several smaller religious statues have also been uncovered (Gray 2013).

The excavators also found dozens of limestone sarcophagi on the seafloor. In ancient Egypt, a sarcophagus was the stone vessel that held the deceased's coffin. The sarcophagi of some of the New Kingdom kings could be quite elaborate, but the ones discovered in the ruins of Heracleion were too small for human bodies, so it is believed they once held animal mummies (Gray 2013). The ancient Egyptians always revered certain animals as sacred, with falcons, ibises, cats, dogs, and crocodiles being among the most sacred, and after the 7th century BCE they began regularly mummifying sacred animals (Shaw and Nicholson 1995, 248). The period when Heracleion was built and at the peak of its influence coincided with the popular trend of animal mummification in Egypt, so the small sarcophagi discovered there would certainly make sense.

Along with the important religious artifacts that have been uncovered in Heracleion, many items that attest to the city's economic importance and position as a central port have also been discovered. Goddio believes that there were more than 60 shipwrecks in the Heracleion harbor from the 6th century BCE to the 2nd century CE, a theory supported by the discovery of more than 700 ancient anchors on the seafloor (Goddio 2018a). A number of smaller maritime items have also been excavated along with the anchors, which further solidifies the image of Heracleion being a bustling city in its prime. As ships made their way to Heracleion from the Mediterranean Sea and the Nile River, some of the extra traffic was probably sent to Naucratis and Canopus, but apparently the harbor masters could not always control the traffic and accidents happened. Unfortunately, there is not yet enough information to conclusively determine how the harbor functioned and how the temples operated. In the absence of historical texts that offer more details, Egyptologists are left to synthesize the findings by Goddio and his team with known temple and harbor activities from other Egyptian cities to create an image of what life in Heracleion must have looked like. There are plenty of known examples concerning the functions of temples to draw conclusions about the Amun-Gereb Temple and the Khonsu sanctuary, assuming the temples would have worked much in the same way as any other temple in Egypt. Reconstructing how the harbor functioned may be a bit more difficult since Heracleion was so unique compared to other ancient Egyptian cities, but there are some later historical references that help bring a little more clarity.

Goddio and other scholars who have worked on reconstructing Heracleion, both archaeologically and in terms of ancient Egyptian chronology, agree that the city first came to prominence during the Twenty-Sixth Dynasty. Although a settlement may have been there before the Twenty-Sixth Dynasty, Heracleion became a major port city along with Naucratis and Canopus in the late 7th century BCE. As Goddio noted, "all trade had to go through the city," (Sooke 2016) so its growth was inevitable. The native population would have been supplemented by Greek and Phoenician traders whose numbers could have been significant at any given time. After the Twenty-Sixth Dynasty, the city continued to grow and probably reached its peak just before the Ptolemies took control of Egypt.

Conclusion

As this ongoing work suggests, the work of Egyptologists continues to uncover more artifacts, and historians learn more about antiquity by the day. Born in the Nile Valley over 5,000 years ago, Egyptian culture was rediscovered by the efforts of scholars from both Britain and France, but Egyptology was quickly expanded by the efforts of others from a host of nations. German scholar Richard Lepsius led the first major German expedition into Egypt from 1842-1845, which led to a long and fruitful German influence in Egyptology (Reid 2004, 46), and today most Egyptological scholarly journals allow article submissions in English, French, and German, a testament to the international scope in which the study began and remains to this day. Americans came much later to the study of Egyptology, but by the end of the 19th century they also made great strides in the discipline. Three of the most vital scholars in American Egyptology – George Reisner, James Henry Breasted, and Albert Lythgoe – learned the craft in German universities (Reid 2004, 199), and these men led significant archeological expeditions in Egypt that helped build the significant collections of Egyptian antiquities at the Boston Museum of Fine Arts, New York City's Metropolitan Museum of Art, the University of Pennsylvania's Museum, the Brooklyn Museum, and the Oriental Institute of the University of Chicago. By the middle of the 20th century, scores of museums in Western Europe, Canada, the United States, and Australia possessed significant collections of Egyptian antiquities, while dozens of academic programs in those same countries taught aspiring Egyptologists the fundamentals of ancient Egyptian grammar, history, and archeology.

Of course, the expansion of Egyptology was not limited to traditional Western countries. As the discipline of Egyptology spread throughout the West, and as the West expanded its influence throughout the entire world during the 19th and 20th centuries, it was perhaps inevitable that Egyptology would be picked up in traditionally non-Western countries. In South America, Argentina, Uruguay, and Brazil all have societies dedicated to the study of ancient Egypt (Jeffreys 2011, 15), and new departments are being created in universities where South American students can learn from established experts in the field.

Even if those South American countries are now considered "Western" by many of their inhabitants, other traditionally non-Western countries have also made recent significant forays into Egyptology. When the former Soviet Union first developed close ties with the modern state of Egypt during the construction of the Aswan dam in the 1950s, it established an archeological presence in the Nile Valley (Jeffreys 2011, 15). More recently, China and Japan have also established societies for the study of ancient Egypt and have conducted archaeological research in Egypt (Jeffreys 2011, 15-16). The worldwide trend appears to have Egyptology moving towards a more international study instead of one that is dominated by traditionally Western countries.

Why does the fascination with ancient Egypt continue to grow and become a global phenomenon? Perhaps the answer to that question can be found with the original enigma that the Egyptian hieroglyphic script presented to the world, which the Rosetta Stone helped solve. Despite the fact that much more is known about Egypt today thanks to the deciphering of the Rosetta Stone, the Nile Valley continues to hold an aura of mystery more than any other location on the planet, at least when it comes to ancient culture. As David Wengrow put it, "The contradictions and paradoxes implicit in the Napoleonic encounter with Ancient Egypt remain with us, in the uneasy coexistence of Egyptology with a strong public desire to retain a source of mystery, sensuous experience and self-knowledge. They are also manifest in the ambiguous place which Egyptology itself continues to occupy between the humanities and the social sciences. The name given to the study of Egypt (like Assyri-*ology* and anthrop-*ology*) incorporates it into a field of knowledge conceived as a scientific study of the 'other', but often practised as the humanistic search for 'self.'" (Wengrow 2011, 192-93).

Appendix: A Full List of Members of the *Commission des Sciences et des Arts*

Pierre-Onésime Adnès the elder (1760–1819), mechanic

Simon-Onésime Adnès, (1780–1820), mechanic

François Sébastien Aimé (1762–1843), mechanic

Bertrand Alibert (1775–1808), polytechnician (X 1794), engineer of the Ponts et Chaussées

Felice Ansiglioni, printer (Oriental section)

Antoine-Vincent Arnault (1766–1834), writer

Pierre Arnollet (1776–1857), polytechnician (X 1796), engineer of the Ponts et Chaussées

Charles-Louis Balzac (1752–1820), architect

Pierre Joseph de Beauchamp (1752–1801), astronomer and diplomat

Beaudoin, printer (French section)

B. Belletête (1778–1808), orientalist and interpreter

Denis Samuel Bernard (1776–1853), polytechnician (X 1794), engineer of the Ponts et Chaussées

Claude Louis Berthollet (1748–1822), chemist

Jacques Antoine Bertre (1776–1834), polytechnician (X 1794), geographical engineer

Julien Bessières (1777–1840), surgeon

Besson, printer (French section)

Louis Victor Bodard (1765–1799), engineer of the Ponts et Chaussées

A.-N.-F. Bonjean (1775–1845), marine engineer

Mathurin-François Boucher (1778–1851), polytechnician (X 1794), ingénieur du génie maritime

Jean-Baptiste Pierre Boudet (1748–1828), pharmacist in chief

Boulanger, printer (French section)

L. S. Bourgeois

Boyer, printer (French section)

Damien Bracevich (died 1830), interpreter

Maximilien de Caffarelli du Falga, general

Caquet (died 1799), artist

Philippe Joseph Marie Caristie (1775–1852), polytechnicien (X 1794), engineer of the Ponts et Chaussées

Jean-Jacques Castex (1731–1822), sculptor

François-Charles Cécile (1766–1840), mechanic

comte Jacques Joseph Gaspard Antoine Chabrol de Volvic (1773–1843), polytechnician (X 1794), engineer of the Ponts et Chaussées

père Jacques-Pierre Champy (1744–1816), chemist

Nicolas Champy (1776–1801), polytechnicien (X 1794), chemist

Jean-Siméon Champy (1778–1845), polytechnicien (X 1794), gunpowder commissaire

Jean François Chaumont (1774–1856), polytechnicien (X 1795), marine engineer

Callixte-Victor Cirot (died 1801), mechanic

Jean Colin (died 1801), mechanic

H. V. Collet-Descotils (1773–1815), chemist

Nicolas-Jacques Conté (1755–1805), director of mechanics

Ernest Coquebert de Monbret (1780–1801), botanist

Jean Baptiste Corabœuf (1777–1859), polytechnician (X 1794), capitaine en premier dans le corps des ingénieurs géographes

Louis Alexandre de Corancez (1770–1832), geometer

Pierre Louis Antoine Cordier (1777–1861), mineralogist

Louis Costaz (1767–1842), geometer

Jean-Marie-Joseph Coutelle (1748–1835), adjunct to the director of mechanics

Couvreur, mechanic

Jacques-Denis Delaporte (1777–1861), orientalist

Dominique Vivant Denon (1747–1825), writer, artist

Desfours, mechanic

J. Dewèvre (1775–1799), surgeon

Déodat Gratet de Dolomieu (1750–1801), mineralogist and geologist

G. de Dominicis, printer (Oriental section)

Antoine Dubois (1756–1837), doctor

Isidore Dubois (born 1782), surgeon

Nicolas Dubois (born 1776), polytechnician (X 1794), printer (French section)

Jean-Marie Dubois-Aymé (1779–1846), engineer of the Ponts et Chaussées

Louis Duchanoy (1781–1847), engineer of the Ponts et Chaussées

Jacques Auguste Dulion (1776–1798), polytechnician (X 1795)

Victor Dupuis (1777–1861), polytechnician (X 1794), ingénieur géographe

André Dutertre (1753–1842), painter

Léonard Duval (1768–1798), engineer of the Ponts et Chaussées

Ch. M. Eberhardt (born 1782), printer (French section)

Elias Fatalla, head of the printer (Oriental section)

J.-P. Faurie (1760–1799), geographical engineer

Louis Joseph Favier (1776–1855), polytechnician (X 1796), engineer of the Ponts et Chaussées

Hervé Charles Antoine Faye (1763–1825), engineer of the Ponts et Chaussées

J.-L. Féraud (1750–1809)

Jean Baptiste Simon Fèvre (1775–1850), polytechnician (X 1794), engineer of the Ponts et Chaussées

Pierre Denis Fouquet, artist

Joseph Fourier (1768–1830), geometer

Antoine Galland (1763–1851), printer (French section)

Étienne Geoffroy Saint-Hilaire (1772–1844), naturalist

Alexandre Sébastien Gérard (1779–1853), polytechnician (X 1798), naturalist

Pierre-Simon Girard (1765–1835), chief engineer of the Ponts et Chaussées

Alexis Gloutier (1758–1800), administrator

Philippe Greslé (1776–1846), polytechnician (X 1795), shipbuilder

Jean Charles Hassenfratz (1766–1834), mechanic

François Michel Hérault (died 1800), mechanic

Jean-Baptiste Hochu (born 1775), mechanic

Pierre Jacotin (1765–1827), geographical engineer

Jardin, printer (French section)

Pierre Amédée Jaubert (1779–1847), orientalist and interpreter

Jean-Baptiste Prosper Jollois (1776–1842), polytechnician (X 1794), engineer of the Ponts et Chaussées, entrusted with the hydraulic works in the Nile Delta

Louis Auguste Joly (1774–1798), painter

Edme François Jomard (1777–1862), polytechnician (X 1794), geographical engineer and archaeologist

Jean-Baptiste Jomard (1780–1868), student geographical engineer

Jean Joseph Labâte (1766–1835), doctor

Jean-Baptiste Lacipière (born 1776), surgeon

Michel Ange Lancret (1774–1807), polytechnician (X 1794), engineer of the Ponts et Chaussées

X. Laporte (died 1799), printer (French section)

François Laroche (1778–1806), polytechnician (X 1795), geographical engineer

Le Brun (died 1801)

Bienheureux Lecesne (1772–1827), geographical engineer

Louis Marie Leduc (born 1772), antiquary

Pierre Eustache Leduc (died 1799), geographical engineer

Marie Jules César Lelorgne de Savigny (1777–1851), zoologist

Lenoble, interprètre

Pierre Lenoir (1776–1827), mechanic

Jean-Baptiste Lepère (1761–1844), architect

Gratien Le Père (1769–1832), chief engineer of the Ponts et Chaussées

Jacques-Marie Le Père (1763–1841), chief engineer of the Ponts et Chaussées

Lerouge (died 1801), chemist

Lethioux, printer (French section)

J. F. L. Levesque (born 1760), geographical engineer

Santi Jean-Baptiste L'Homaca, interpreter

Amable Nicolas Lhomond (1770–1854), mechanic

F. Maccagni (1763–1846), printer (Oriental section)

Jean-Joseph Marcel (1776–1854), director of printers

Marlet, printer (French section)

Pierre-Denis Martin (1771–1855), engineer of the Ponts et Chaussées

Jérôme Isaac Méchain (1778–1851), astronome

Antonio Mesabki, imprimeur section orientale

Benoît Marie Moline de Saint-Yon (1780–1842), polytechnician (X 1794), engineer of the Ponts et Chaussées

Gaspard Monge, comte de Péluse (1746–1818), mathematician

Hippolyte Nectoux (1759–1836), botanist

Charles Norry (1756–1832), architect

Nicolas-Antoine Nouet (1740–1811), astronomer

Panhusen (died 1798), orientalist and interpreter

François-Auguste Parseval-Grandmaison (1759–1834), writer

L. Pellegrini, printer (Oriental section)

Charles Plazanet (1773–1868), mechanic

Paul Nicaise Pottier (1778–1842), polytechnician (X 1794), engineer of the Ponts et Chaussées

Roland Victor Pottier (1775- ?), polytechnician (X 1795), ingénieur géographe

François Pouqueville (1770–1838), surgeon

Pourlier, antiquary

Jean Constantin Protain (1769–1837), architect

J.-J. Puntis (1758–1812), printer (French section)

François Marie Quenot (born 1761), astronomer

Alire Raffeneau-Delile (1778–1850), botanist

Adrien Raffeneau-Delile (1773–1843), engineer of the Ponts et Chaussées

Louis Rémy Raige (1777–1810), orientalist

Henri-Joseph Redouté (1766–1852), painter

Michel-Louis-Étienne Regnaud de Saint-Jean d'Angély (1762–1819), politician

Joseph Angélique Sébastien Regnault (1776–1823), polytechnicien (X 1794), engineer of the Ponts et Chaussées, adjunct to Bertholet and entrusted with controlling the currency in Cairo

G. Renno (1777–1848), printer (Oriental section)

Henri Jean Rigel (1772–1852), compositor

Michel Rigo (1770–1815), painter

Louis Ripault (1775–1823), antiquary

Rivet, printer (French section)

Alexandre Roguin (born 1771), pharmacist

N. Roselli, printer (French section)

Pierre Charles Rouyer (1769–1831), pharmacist

François Michel de Rozière (1773–1842), mining engineer

Ruga, printer (Oriental section)

Alexandre de Saint-Genis (1772–1834), polytechnician (X 1794), engineer of the Ponts et Chaussées

André Louis de Saint-Simon (died 1799), knight of Malta

Pierre Simonel (died 1810), geographical engineer

Jean-Lambert Tallien (1767–1820), National Convention member

Dominique Testevuide (1735–1798), chief geographical engineer

Claude François Thévenod (1772–1798), polytechnicien (X 1794), engineer of the Ponts et Chaussées

Jean Michel de Venture de Paradis (1739–1799), chief interpreter

Very, printer (French section)

Jacques Antoine Viard (1783–1849), student of the École nationale des ponts et chaussées

René Édouard de Villiers du Terrage (1780–1855), polytechnician (X 1794), inspector general of the Ponts et Chaussées, employed in leveling the Suez isthmus

Guillaume André Villoteau (1759–1839), musicographer

Jean Pierre Séraphin Vincent (1779–1818), polytechnician (X 1796), marine engineer

Louis Vincent (born 1780), engineer of the Ponts et Chaussées

Online Resources

Other Egyptian history titles by Charles River Editors

Other titles about Egyptology on Amazon

Further Reading

Adkins, Roy; Adkins, Lesley (2006). The War for All the Oceans. Abacus. ISBN 978-0-349-11916-8.

Allen, Joseph (1905 [1842]). Battles of the British Navy. Simpkin, Marshall, Hamilton, Kent & Co.

Baker, Margaret (1995). London Statues and Monuments. Shire Publications Ltd. ISBN 0-7478-0284-X.

Bradford, Ernle (1999 [1977]). Nelson: The Essential Hero. Wordsworth Military Library. ISBN 1-84022-202-6.

Castex, Jean-Claude (2003). Dictionnaire des batailles navales franco-anglaises. Les Presses de l'Université Laval. ISBN 2-7637-8061-X.

Chandler, David (1999 [1993]). Dictionary of the Napoleonic Wars. Wordsworth Military Library. ISBN 1-84022-203-4.

Clowes, William Laird (1997 [1900]). The Royal Navy, A History from the Earliest Times to 1900, Volume IV. Chatham Publishing. ISBN 1-86176-013-2.

Cole, Juan (2007). Napoleon's Egypt; Invading the Middle East. Palgrave Macmillan. ISBN 978-1-4039-6431-1.

Forester, C.S. (2001 [1929]). Nelson. Chatham Publishing. ISBN 1-86176-178-3.

Gardiner, Robert, ed (2001 [1996]). Nelson Against Napoleon. Caxton Editions. ISBN 1-86176-026-4

Germani, Ian (January 2000). "Combat and Culture: Imagining the Battle of the Nile". The Northern Mariner X (1): 53–72.

Ingram, Edward (July 1984). "Illusions of Victory: The Nile, Copenhagen, and Trafalgar Revisited". Military Affairs 48 (3): 140–143.

James, William (2002 [1827]). The Naval History of Great Britain, Volume 2, 1797–1799. Conway Maritime Press. ISBN 0-85177-906-9.

Jordan, Gerald; Rogers, Nicholas (July 1989). "Admirals as Heroes: Patriotism and Liberty in Hanoverian England". The Journal of British Studies 28 (3): 201–224.

Keegan, John (2003). Intelligence in War: Knowledge of the Enemy from Napoleon to Al-Qaeda. Pimlico. ISBN 0-7126-6650-8.

Maffeo, Steven E. (2000). Most Secret and Confidential: Intelligence in the Age of Nelson. London: Chatham Publishing. ISBN 1-86176-152-X.

Mostert, Noel (2007). The Line upon a Wind: The Greatest War Fought at Sea Under Sail 1793–1815. Vintage Books. ISBN 978-0-7126-0927-2.

Musteen, Jason R. (2011). Nelson's Refuge: Gibraltar in the Age of Napoleon. Naval Investiture Press. ISBN 978-1-59114-545-5.

Padfield, Peter (2000 [1976]). Nelson's War. Wordsworth Military Library. ISBN 1-84022-225-5.

Rodger, N.A.M. (2004). The Command of the Ocean. Allan Lane. ISBN 0-7139-9411-8.

Rose, J. Holland (1924). "Napoleon and Sea Power". Cambridge Historical Journal 1 (2): 138–157.

Smith, Digby (1998). The Napoleonic Wars Data Book. Greenhill Books. ISBN 1-85367-276-9

Warner, Oliver (1960). The Battle of the Nile. London: B. T. Batsford.

Woodman, Richard (2001). The sea warriors: fighting captains and frigate warfare in the age of Nelson. London: Constable. ISBN 1-84119-183-3

Free Books by Charles River Editors

We have brand new titles available for free most days of the week. To see which of our titles are currently free, click on this link.

Discounted Books by Charles River Editors

We have titles at a discount price of just 99 cents everyday. To see which of our titles are currently 99 cents, <u>click on this link</u>.

Printed in Great Britain
by Amazon